NORTHWEST HOMEGROWN COOKBOOK SERIES

Stone Fruit

CYNTHIA NIMS

ILLUSTRATED BY DON BARNETT

Cherries   Nectarines   Apricots   Plums   Peaches

WestWinds Press®

This volume of the Northwest Homegrown Cookbook Series is dedicated to

all the farmers in the Northwest who follow their hearts, work the land, and gamble

with Mother Nature to bring outstanding seasonal fruits to our markets and to

our kitchens. Without them, our lives would not be quite so sweet.

Text © 2003 by Cynthia Nims
Illustrations © 2003 by Don Barnett

Library of Congress Cataloging-in-Publication Data

Nims, Cynthia C.
   Stone fruit : cherries, nectarines, apricots, plums, peaches / by Cynthia Nims.
     p. cm. — (Northwest homegrown cookbook series)
   ISBN 1-55868-602-9
   1. Cookery (Stone fruit) I. Title. II. Series.
  TX813.S85N56 2003
  641.6'42—dc21

2002155537

WestWinds Press®
An imprint of Graphic Arts Center Publishing Company
P.O. Box 10306, Portland, Oregon 97296-0306
503-226-2402
www.gacpc.com

President: Charles M. Hopkins
Associate Publisher: Douglas A. Pfeiffer
Editorial Staff: Timothy W. Frew, Tricia Brown, Kathy Howard, Jean Andrews, Jean Bond-Slaughter
Production Staff: Richard L. Owsiany, Susan Dupere
Editor: Ellen Wheat
Designer: Elizabeth Watson

Printed in Hong Kong

Mention of the Pacific Northwest evokes powerful imagery, from the region's rugged ocean coast to massive mountain peaks, dense forests, and lush valleys, and to the rolling hills beyond. This topography, along with dynamic Pacific weather patterns, creates the climate that, in turn, drives our seasonal rhythms—indeed, four distinct seasons. From the damp, mild coastal areas to the more extreme arid land east of the Cascade Mountains, the growing regions of the Northwest yield a boggling array of foods. The Northwest—from Alaska and British Columbia to Washington, Idaho, Oregon, and Northern California—is a top national producer of apples, lentils, hops, hazelnuts, plums, peppermint, sweet onions, potatoes, and many types of berries. The ocean, bays,

and rivers supply the region with a broad selection of fish and shellfish, and rain-soaked foothills give us prized wild mushrooms.

For the Northwest cook, this wealth of ingredients means ready access to mouthwatering edibles such as morels and asparagus with halibut in spring, rich salmon with peaches and raspberries during summer, delicious pears, chanterelles, and cranberries harvested in fall, and plump oysters and mussels in winter.

The distinctive bounty of our regional foods makes for a culinary landscape that is as compelling as the natural landscape. This series of Northwest Homegrown Cookbooks shines the spotlight on those individual foods that flourish seasonally in this place that I call home. Savor this taste of the Northwest.

ACKNOWLEDGMENTS

Much of the pleasure in working on this book came from talking with and visiting fruit growers, who shared with me not only their firsthand knowledge of the fruits, their seasons and particularities, but also the sense of dedication and passion that they have for tending their orchards and growing the best fruit they can. These men and women share a kinship with generations of Northwesterners before them, all of whom have made the industry of stone fruit a significant piece of this region's history and development, the story I'm pleased to share with you here. Among the many growers who shared their time and expertise with me are Bert Pence at Pence Orchards in Wapato, Washington; Holly Douglas at Douglas Fruit in Pasco, Washington; Susan Putman at Inland–Joseph Fruit Company also in Wapato; Lee Schrepel at Fruithill in Yamhill, Oregon; and Ron Lawrence at R & R Farms in Wenatchee, Washington.

Many thanks, too, to John Fellman, associate professor of postharvest physiology in the Department of Horticulture and Landscape Architecture at Washington State University; Robert McGorrin, head of the Department of Food Science and Technology at Oregon State University; Eric Patrick at the Washington State Fruit Commission; and Mary Stewart, executive director of the Agri-Business Council of Oregon.

I so appreciate help from food-science maven Shirley Corriher, who can make the study of how pectin works sound like an exciting tale of adventure. And thanks also to Kristine Britton for her help with recipe testing and research.

Recipe testers and tasters are an important part of creating recipes that are as doable and delicious as they can be, so I must thank my dear sister Barbara Nims, Ed Silver, Michael Amend, Jeff Ashley, Anne Nisbet, Joanne Koonce-Hamar, Tim and Katherine Kehrli, Cynthia Daste, Gillian Allen-White, Sephi Coyle, and Andy Jellin, not to mention the many taster-critics who came to dinner.

CONTENTS

Breakfast/Brunch 17

Appetizers, Salads, and Side Dishes 33

Main Courses 45

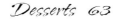

Desserts 63

Beverages 77

Cooking with Stone Fruit 86

Introduction

Imagine biting into a perfect peach: the aroma wafts to your nose at the moment your teeth penetrate the soft fruit while the intense, juicy flavor rolls over your tongue, the nectar bursting out and dribbling down to your elbows. It's an experience that won't happen in April or February or November, but only during a handful of summertime weeks when the fruit is at its peak of ripeness.

Welcome to the wonderful world of stone fruit. Not a sexy moniker to be sure, but this group of fruits does include some of the most ambrosial foods known to man. It's no coincidence that the nectarine takes its name from the Greek word *nektar* referring to the drink of the gods. Or that when life is good, it's said to be just a bowl of cherries, or plum-dandy, or peachy. The association these fruits have with summer is so keen that their flavors and aromas are almost literally sunny. The ethereal nature of stone fruit is all the more reason that Northwesterners go nuts when the first cherries begin showing up in early June, bringing with them the promise of our few months of luscious fruit to enjoy while we can.

Stone fruits are those that have a single hard pit, or stone: peaches, nectarines, apricots, plums, and cherries. Such fruits are also known as drupes, which classifies a broader family that includes almonds and pecans among others. In the latter two examples, the hard shell we crack to get at the nut is comparable to the pit of a peach, which also has a nut—actually a seed—inside. (The pits and seeds of stone fruit are toxic, though, and are not considered edible. They contain concentrations of hydrocyanic acid or cyanide.) What we rarely see in an almond is the fleshy covering, technically the mesocarp, that covers it, discarded in nut processing but the raison d'être of its fruity cousins.

Throughout the Northwest, from the Okanagan Valley of British Columbia to the north-central valleys of California and east into Idaho, stone fruit is abundant. The Pacific Coast states together produce most, if not nearly all, of the United States' sweet cherries, apricots, peaches, nectarines, and plums. In the last fifty years or so, the major growing regions in the United States have been shifting from the east to the west. Today, the importance of stone fruit in the Northwest is significant. Washington, Oregon, and Northern California together produce 90 percent or more of the country's

sweet cherries, apricots, plums, and nectarines, and roughly 75 percent of the nation's peaches. Though stone fruits grow quite well in many backyards and small orchards west of the Cascades, the bulk of production is in the interior regions where weather conditions are ideal.

No amount of agricultural advancement or transportation marvels will alter the fact that the season for stone fruit is a fleeting one. It is the nature of the fruits themselves, their composition and how they ripen. The best of the region's fruit is picked when it is fully mature and just on the verge of its peak flavor and texture. It is these fruits that Northwesterners are after when they hop in the car and drive to Oregon's Hood River Valley, to Wenatchee, Washington, or to British Columbia's Okanagan Valley, buying up boxes of tree-ripe fruit so they can cook up an embarrassment of summertime recipes, or can, or share with friends and neighbors, though not until they've first eaten their fill in the parking lot before leaving the fruit stand. The forty recipes in the following pages will help you make the most of these delicious fruits of our Northwest summers.

The Story of Northwest Stone Fruit

A Brief History

The Oregon Trail was the path by which most of the region's European settlers arrived in the western reaches of what is now the United States. One homesteader in particular, Henderson Luelling, came from Iowa with his family in 1847 and had a singular impact on the region's agricultural development. But even earlier, settlers found their way to the Pacific Northwest and began the first cultivation of fruit in the region.

John McLoughlin, a chief factor for the Hudson's Bay Company, arrived in 1825, founding Fort Vancouver on the banks of the Columbia River and establishing a trading center that quickly grew to meet demands of the burgeoning region. The first peaches grown in the Oregon Territory are said to be sprouted pits that were brought to Fort Vancouver and given to McLoughlin by a sailor in 1829. The sailor had collected the peaches on Juan Fernandez Island (off the coast of Chile, since renamed Robinson Crusoe Island). McLoughlin was also given apple and grape seeds in 1825 by Captain Simpson, who had carried them on a trip that originated in London. But it would be two decades before other fruits would come to the region and the industry of fruit culture would begin to flourish.

When homesteader Henderson Luelling (also spelled Lewelling) and his family followed the Oregon Trail from Iowa, they were in what has been called the million-dollar wagon train. The trip was already treacherous enough with challenges of weather and natural obstacles, not to mention provisioning a six-month journey, but Luelling added to that the transport of hundreds of fruit tree and vine seedlings in two specially designed wagons.

Tending to the seedlings en route and assuring their safe passage only added to the stresses of the trek, but his determination and care paid off. Luelling is said to have arrived with cherries, plums, grapes, berries, apples, and black walnut trees among his collection. Along with brother Seth, Luelling settled near what is now Milwaukie, just outside Portland, Oregon, and established what would soon be a thriving nursery and orchard. Chroniclers later estimated the eventual value of those Oregon Trail seedlings to be in the neighborhood of one million dollars.

California's early settlement and development came from the south, with the expansion of the Spanish territories northward from Mexico. Fruit and other agricultural crops made their way to this area with Spanish settlers who planted orchards at missions as far back as the late eighteenth century. Apricots are among the earliest fruits mentioned in historical documents, with other stone fruits apparently appearing later in the nineteenth century as California's agricultural valleys were settled and exploited.

Substantial fruit production in California helped fuel the development of canneries in the late 1800s, particularly in San Francisco with its direct access to rail and sea transport. The earthquake and resulting fire that devastated San Francisco in 1906 wiped out a number of canneries that had been established in the city. By 1907, a large new cannery had been built on the San Francisco waterfront and, by 1909, it was the largest fruit and vegetable cannery in the world, much of that production in peaches and apricots. This California Fruit Cannery Association would eventually join forces with other fruit producers and become California Packers Association (Calpak, for short). Finally, in 1967, the company changed its name to Del Monte, though the Del Monte name had been used since early in the twentieth century, denoting the premier products of the cannery.

Fur trapping and gold mining drew the first non-Native settlers to the Okanagan Valley of British Columbia beginning in the early nineteenth century. With them came some of the first fruit trees grown in the region, though more significant plantings would come later as larger settlements were established. On the sunny western shore of Okanagan Lake is Summerland, named to reflect the distinctive warm microclimate of this northern valley, where the Canadian government established the Pacific Agri-Food Research Centre in 1914. This laboratory was established with the primary goal of deciding which crops (and livestock breeds) were best suited to the area and to research methods for optimizing their production. The ornamental gardens and first orchards of the Canadian Okanagan were planted in 1916. The Van cherry, released in 1944, was one of the research program's key developments, and today their cherry breeding program is still very active.

Growing Regions

The temperate regions of the inland valleys of Washington, Oregon, California, and British Columbia have ideal growing conditions for stone fruit. These areas have in common a major north-south mountain range to the west, which produces a rain-shadow effect, leaving the eastern side of the mountains with a relatively dry climate and hot summers to promote full development and ripening of the fruit.

Chill plays an important role too, though; the freezing temperatures of winter are important for dormancy, which promotes the optimal flower development the following spring. Moderation is important, however, because temperatures that dip too low or last too long can leave permanent damage, severely limiting the year's harvest. The happy medium that these Northwestern regions provide—the balance between hot but not too hot summers and cold but not too cold winters, plus plenty of irrigation and naturally rich soil—is ideal for bountiful fruit production.

In Washington and British Columbia, the defining mountain range is the Cascades, with most of the region's production east of the Cascades, in the Okanagan Valley in British Columbia, and the Columbia River Basin and Yakima Valley in Washington. The Okanagan Valley is one of the warmest, driest parts of all Canada, making its significance as a fruit (and wine-grape) growing region even greater. Peaches and cherries are among the more important crops grown there.

Oregon splits its fruit production somewhat. The Hood River area to the east of the Cascades produces primarily apricots, peaches, nectarines, and sweet cherries for the fresh market, while the Willamette and Yamhill Valleys to the west, nestled between the coast range and the Cascades, produces the bulk of the state's plums and cherries destined for processing.

California has a vast agricultural valley between the coast ranges and the Sierra Nevada that is home to crops as varied as avocados, strawberries, lemons, broccoli, onions, and artichokes. The agricultural core of this area is the Central Valley, and the northern half of this valley is where the bulk of the state's stone fruit is grown. Even farther inland, the southwestern region of Idaho is where that state's sweet cherry, peach, and plum orchards flourish.

Northwest Stone Fruit Varieties and Seasonality

Sweet Cherries. Sweet cherries are the premier stone fruit of the Northwest, with recent USDA statistics showing the annual value of this one fruit to be in the neighborhood of $270 million, a generous half of the value of all the region's stone fruit varieties combined. In Canada, the Okanagan Valley area produces more than three-quarters of the nation's sweet cherries.

There are three basic types of Northwest cherries: sweet cherries for the fresh market, sweet cherries for production, and sour cherries (also known as tart or pie cherries). Sour cherries make up a small percentage of the region's cherry harvest and virtually all of it goes into commercial production (as for cherry pie filling). The state of Michigan reigns on our continent where sour cherries are concerned, but the Northwest is where it's at for those plump sweet cherries of summer.

The fresh cherry market is dominated by the Bing cherry, developed in the Oregon orchards of pioneer Northwest fruit grower Seth Luelling and named for one of his Chinese orchard workers. This large dark-skinned cherry with deep red, juicy flesh is the quintessential cherry of the region. Other dark sweet varieties include the Lambert (developed in the Luelling orchards by Joseph Hamilton Lambert in 1870), the Lapin (developed in the early 1980s at the Summerland Research Station in British Columbia), the Chelan (developed in the 1970s in Prosser by Washington State University researchers), the Sweetheart (released at Summerland in 1994), and the Van (developed at Summerland in the 1940s).

Rainier cherries are among the most prized, a firm-fleshed sweet cherry with pale flesh and yellow skin with a red blush. This large cherry was developed at the Washington State University research station in Prosser, Washington, by Dr. Harold Fogle, crossing the Bing and Van cherries. It is one of the prime export cherries for the region; Asian buyers in particular are very taken with the lovely, juicy Rainier cherry.

One sweet cherry variety that Henderson Luelling transported from Iowa was the blush Napoleon Bigarreau cherry, which he renamed (for reasons unknown) the Royal Ann. The Royal Ann went on to become one of the most profitable cherry varieties in the Northwest. We rarely see this cherry fresh in markets. Most of the harvest instead is used for the nation's maraschino cherry industry, which also has roots in Oregon (see page 81).

As with all stone fruit, the season for cherries varies depending on the variety, the growing area, and the weather conditions any given year. In general, the year's first cherries (including Chelan and Bing) are harvested in Northern California as early as mid-May, and the picking progresses northward with the warming temperatures. Later varieties, such as Sweetheart, reach their peak in August in the Okanagan Valley. I have found late-summer stone fruit rapture with a trip to Vancouver's Granville Island market, to bask in the late-season bounty of those orchards to the north.

Peaches. Though peaches are a distant second to cherries in economic impact on the Pacific Northwest, this fruit holds its own as one of the most iconic summertime treats. There are dozens of peach varieties grown in California, Washington, Oregon, Idaho, and British Columbia, including Red Haven, Rosa, Summer Lady, Flavorcrest, O'Henry, and Suncrest. As is true with most stone fruit, different varieties have different maturing times, which allows picking cycles to overlap so growers can draw out their peach season for several months. The prime season for most Northwest peaches is July and August.

Douglas Fruit in Pasco, Washington, is one of the key Northwest peach growers. Their orchards alone feature about twenty-five varieties of peaches, from the Rich Lady, which begins harvest in early July, continuing through late September with the Yukon King peaches. Fourth-generation grower Holly Douglas points out that on her farm, they tend small blocks of two to eighteen acres per variety. Because of the overlapping maturity of the different types, they're seldom harvesting more than five or six varieties at a time. The trick is that they handpick this fruit "tree ripe" and all the peaches on a tree don't ripen at the same time, so the pickers will pass through a given block four or five times over the course of a couple of weeks.

Though a perfectly ripe yellow peach is a joy in itself, there are a few other types of peaches available. White-fleshed peaches are simply a subset of the peach family that produces white flesh rather than yellow. The skin color and other characteristics tend to be similar to yellow peaches, though the flesh is typically a bit sweeter. The donut peach, so named because its flattened form somewhat resembles a doughnut, is a variety of white peach, quite sweet and something of a novelty. And a new generation of subacid peaches has been developed that has lower levels of acidity at maturity, allowing the sweetness of the fruit to be even more pronounced. These innovative peach varieties tend to have telling names, such as Country Sweet, Sweet Dream, and Joanna Sweet.

Nectarines. Most of the characteristics of the nectarine echo those of the peach, though not quite as many varieties are grown and the overall season isn't quite as long. The common belief is that the nectarine is simply a fuzzless peach, and the fruit is in fact very closely related to the peach. But nectarines aren't just a modern variation on the peach created in a researcher's lab. Their origins go back a couple thousand years to Asia. Among the best-known nectarine varieties that are harvested in the Northwest are Supreme Red, Candy Gold, Independence, Fireburst, and Sun Glo.

In Northwest orchards, nectarines are typically available from early July through mid-September, with both yellow- and white-fleshed varieties in stores and at farmers markets. With their thin, fuzzless skin, nectarines can be preferable to peaches, because the slightly heavier, fuzzy skin of peaches often needs to be removed while the skin of nectarines can be left on in most recipes.

Apricots. The West Coast grows virtually all of the country's apricots, with north-central California's contribution more than 90 percent and most of the rest coming from Washington State. Up in Canada, it's the Okanagan Valley that again tops the Canadian agricultural statistics, accounting for virtually all of the nation's apricot harvest.

There are a few dozen varieties of brilliant golden-orange apricots grown in the Northwest, including Moorpark, Perfection, Rival, Castlebrite, Tomcot, and Goldbar, with variations in size, texture, and shape that make some better for recipes, others ideal for eating out of hand. Apricots are among the most delicate fruits, so typically the selection and quality is limited at traditional grocery stores. This is one fruit worth seeking out at regional fruit stands and farmers markets for peak ripeness and selection. July is generally the peak season for Northwest apricots.

Plums (and Prunes). There is a lot of confusion surrounding the names used for plums, primarily with regard to exactly what a "prune" is. Is it different from a plum? a type of plum? or simply a generic reference to any dried plum? The answer could just as well be "all of the above," given the inconsistent use of the term *prune*. I prefer to consider that *plum* always refers to a fresh fruit; *prune* is used only for dried fruit.

Prune-plum is occasionally used to refer to plum varieties grown primarily for drying, which helps distinguish them from their plum counterparts when marketed fresh. These fruits, also known as Italian plums, have a higher sugar content than other plums, which makes them well suited to drying because fermentation or decay is impeded by the higher sugar levels. This is not true of all plum varieties. To help curb some of the terminology confusion, the California Prune Board recently renamed their product the dried plum, thus becoming the California Dried Plum Board, perhaps also to shake off the sometimes negative connotations associated with the prune.

The primary California prune-plum variety—which has a royal purple outer skin and amber colored flesh—is an offshoot of La Petite d'Agen, a fruit native to southwest France. It was brought to the region by Frenchman Louis Pellier, one of many mid-nineteenth-century arrivals during California's gold rush. When Pellier's dreams for gold didn't pan out, he returned to what he knew: agriculture. In 1850, he established a plum orchard in the Santa Clara Valley, starting with root stock of the Agen plum brought from his native France.

A couple of decades later, Luther Burbank arrived in California from Massachusetts. He was already a respected plant breeder, having developed the Burbank potato (which was sent to Ireland to help relieve the potato blight crisis and was a predecessor of the now-famous Idaho potato). He also devoted much of the work in his Santa Rosa orchards to fruit. More than one hundred varieties of plums alone can be attributed to Burbank, including the well-known Santa Rosa. He's also the man initially responsible for developing the freestone peach, a fruit that was previously a clingstone.

California dominates plum cultivation in the United States, both in fresh plums and those destined for drying; California's plums fulfill about three-quarters of the *world* production of prunes. Oregon, Washington, and Idaho are major producers of plums as well, and together the four states account for well over 90 percent of the plums grown in the country. Among the dozens of plum varieties are Santa Rosa, Shiro, Damson, Yellow Egg, Elephant Heart, and Scarlet Sun.

About the Recipes

Stone fruits are, by their very physiology, delicate fruits that don't travel too well or keep very long in their fresh, ripe state. It's part of what makes the peak summer season such a thing to celebrate, what makes it impossible to pass up those fragrant piles of fruit in the markets when the short seasons are in full swing. So there is an inherent timeliness for cooking with stone fruits, at least when they're at their best.

There are, however, some good off-season alternatives available commercially, including frozen (cherries and peaches), canned (peaches, plums, cherries, and apricots), and dried (apricots, prunes, and cherries) fruit. Such options increase if you freeze or dry your own fruit, or if you're a canner who "puts up" summer fruit when it is flooding the stores. I have addressed such alternatives where appropriate in the recipes, to help give these recipes year-round appeal. There's no denying that some recipes—such as Deep-Dish Peach Pie and Leg of Lamb with Spicy Cherry Salsa—are best saved for making when the fresh season comes around again.

Cooking with flavorful, fully ripe fruit is tastiest and is assumed in the recipes, though you'll see that some recipes specify "ripe but firm" fruit in cases where the fruit will ideally hold its shape during cooking. But don't be tempted to buy very firm, probably underripe, fruit, which will surely bring unsatisfying flavor to the recipe. Ideally the fruit will have all the characteristics of ripe fruit but be somewhat firm rather than soft to the touch. If such choices are limited, you'll be better off with ripe and tender fruit, which may fall apart in cooking but assures delicious results. For more on the ripeness of stone fruits, see page 87.

Breakfast / Brunch

Dutch Baby with Gingered Apricots

Half the fun of making a Dutch Baby is watching the eggy batter puff up while it bakes—almost impossibly increasing its size before your eyes. Take a peek now and then through the oven window to enjoy the show. Sorry, but no peeking if there's no window: opening the oven door during baking will impede the puff. Be sure to show off the stunning big pancake to your breakfast companions before it begins to settle a matter of moments after coming from the oven.

One of the all-time best ways to serve a Dutch Baby is with nothing more than lemon wedges to squeeze and powdered sugar to shake over the buttery-rich pancake. But the gingery sweet apricots in this recipe make for a flavorful summertime embellishment. Choose fragrant, ripe apricots that aren't too soft, so they'll hold their shape after a bit of cooking with candied ginger. Off-season, use frozen peach slices, thawed and cut into large chunks. A good old well-seasoned cast-iron skillet is, in my opinion, the very best Dutch Baby pan.

½ cup unsalted butter
5 eggs
1¼ cups milk

1¼ cups all-purpose flour
Powdered sugar, for serving

Gingered Apricots

2 tablespoons minced candied
  (crystallized) ginger
¼ cup hot water
¾ pound ripe but firm apricots
2 tablespoons unsalted butter

3 tablespoons apricot jam
  or orange marmalade
1 to 2 tablespoons granulated sugar
  (optional)

Preheat the oven to 425°F.

For the gingered apricots, put the minced ginger in a small bowl, pour the hot water over, and set aside for about 15 minutes.

Pit and quarter the apricots. Melt the butter in a medium skillet over medium heat. Add the apricots and cook, tossing gently, until they are just beginning to soften, 2 to 3 minutes. Add the apricot jam with the candied ginger and its soaking water and bring just

A Taste of History

Though Dutch Baby recipes abound and may seem to have no particular sense of "place," the dish can in fact be traced to the Pacific Northwest, and to Manca's restaurant in Seattle in particular. Manca's was one of the prime Seattle dining destinations in the first half of the twentieth century, along with Rosellini's and Canlis and such restaurants that defined local fine dining of that era. It operated from 1897 (the beginning of the Klondike gold rush) and closed in 1957 when its block in downtown Seattle was leveled to build the Norton Building.

Victor Manca created this dish as a variation on the German pancake, which is made in a similar way but in a large size that takes a while to bake. Manca developed a smaller version that he could serve his guests more expeditiously, going so far as to have specific pans made solely for his Dutch Babies. I have talked with Victor's great-grandson, Mark Manca, about the famous dish. Even today, the original Manca's Dutch Baby recipe is a well-guarded family secret, and Dutch Babies are still a Sunday tradition in his family.

to a boil, stirring gently to soften the jam and evenly mix the ingredients. Simmer gently for 3 to 5 minutes to blend the flavors and reduce the liquid a bit. Taste the sauce, adding sugar to taste if you like. Set aside.

For the Dutch Baby, put the butter in a large heavy, ovenproof skillet, preferably cast-iron, and put it in the oven to preheat the pan and fully melt the butter. While the pan is heating, put the eggs in a blender and blend on high speed for 1 minute. With the motor running, add the milk and flour ¼ cup at a time, alternating, and once all the ingredients have been added, blend for 30 seconds longer. Take the skillet from the oven and slowly, gently pour the batter into the skillet. Bake until well puffed and nicely browned, about 25 minutes. Toward the end of cooking, gently reheat the gingered apricots over medium heat and put them in a serving bowl.

When the Dutch Baby is cooked, transfer the skillet to a trivet on the breakfast table and cut the pancake into wedges to serve, passing the warm gingered apricots separately for your guests to spoon over. Also pass a shaker of powdered sugar for adding a final snowy flourish of sweetness to taste.

Makes 6 servings

Peach Waffles with Maple-Peach Syrup

Peach purée added to the batter in this recipe produces scrumptious waffles that are moist and full of flavor. You could spice up the waffles a bit more, if you like, adding ½ teaspoon ground cinnamon to the dry ingredients for the batter, and adding a cinnamon stick to the syrup to infuse a bit of aromatic flavor into the peach-maple mixture. Off-season, frozen peaches make a good substitute; thaw them completely and pat dry with paper towels so excess liquid doesn't water down the waffle batter.

1¾ cups all-purpose flour

¼ cup sugar

2 teaspoons baking powder

¼ teaspoon freshly ground
   or grated nutmeg

Pinch salt

1 medium peach

1¼ cups milk

¼ cup unsalted butter, melted,
   plus more for waffle iron

3 eggs, separated

Maple-Peach Syrup

2 tablespoons unsalted butter

1 peach

1 cup real maple syrup

1 tablespoon dark rum (optional)

For the maple-peach syrup, peel, pit, and finely chop the peach. Heat the butter in a small saucepan over medium heat. Add the peach and cook, stirring occasionally, until quite soft, mashing the pieces against the sides of the pan with the spoon to create a texture that is thick and slightly chunky, about 10 minutes. Add the maple syrup, with the rum, if using, and stir to evenly mix. Keep the syrup warm over very low heat while making the waffles.

Preheat a waffle iron to medium-high heat.

Sift together the flour, sugar, baking powder, nutmeg, and salt into a large bowl and make a large well in the center. Peel, pit, and coarsely chop the peach, then purée it in a food processor (you should have about ¾ cup purée). In a medium bowl, combine the peach purée with the milk, butter, and egg yolks, whisking to blend evenly. Add the wet ingredients to the dry ingredients and gently stir just to combine.

Whip the egg whites with an electric mixer on high speed until soft peaks form. Add about one-third of the egg whites to the batter and use a rubber spatula to briskly fold them in to lighten the batter, then gently fold in the remaining egg whites.

Lightly butter the waffle iron and pour in a generous ½ cup of the batter (more or less depending on the size of your iron). Close the waffle iron and cook until well browned and crisp, 5 to 7 minutes (generally, steam will have stopped being emitted from the waffle iron). Transfer the cooked waffle to a heatproof plate and keep warm in a low oven while you make the remaining waffles.

Arrange the waffles on individual plates, drizzle with some of the warm maple-peach syrup, and serve right away, passing extra syrup separately.

Makes 6 servings

Pence Orchards

Most consumers don't get to know the grower behind the produce they buy, but for a month or so each year customers at one group of grocery stores in the Puget Sound area get an up-close-and-personal introduction to the Pence family, growers of some of the best-loved peaches in Washington State. When Peach-o-Rama comes to Seattle-area Queen Anne Thriftway stores, shoppers are met at the door with a taste of the day's peak-fresh peaches, and may be greeted by one of the Pences in person or perhaps even get to taste some Pence family recipes made with these prized peaches.

Pence Orchards began in the 1920s, primarily with peach trees. Today, Bert Pence is the fourth-generation orchardist who tends that original plot. Over the years, the selection of fruit grown in these Wapato-area orchards has varied, peaches giving way to apples in the 1950s when the state's apple industry was still young. Then in the 1980s, Bert's father, Tom Pence, had the foresight to realize that too many apple trees were being planted and an overabundance of apples was on the horizon. So the family cut back on apples and returned to their roots with additional peach acreage, today about 45 acres, roughly half of their total acreage.

Variety is not only the spice of life; for farmers it is often the key to success. Given the vagaries of market trends and prices, not to mention the risk each year that weather can take a serious bite out of profits, many orchards manage a range of fruits. Pence Orchards, for instance, also grows outstanding Rainier cherries. The trees are tended with great care to produce fruit that meets the stringent demands of import buyers (especially in Japan), who will pay top prices for large, firm, sweet fruit. In fact, the Pence family has been growing Rainier cherries since the variety's earliest days, before the cherry even had a name. "We might have one of the oldest blocks in the valley," says Bert Pence. They have some acreage of Friar plums as well—not much, but what they have is grown with the same care as the peaches, picked tree ripe and gingerly transported to area markets. Ah, but it is those peaches that have Seattle-area shoppers swooning in the produce aisles. They are the peaches of yesteryear, with all the aroma, juiciness, flavor, and perfection that seem to have been lost in the race to modernize the business of fruit culture and distribution.

So, is this a trend in the making? Can we hope to see tree-ripened, handpicked peaches by the truckload at stores everywhere? Not likely. "Most growers and packing houses just are not able to do this," Bert Pence points out. "The reason we can pick our fruit riper is that we're small and we're able to do our packing right in the orchards." Pickers pluck the peaches from the tree and put them into padded buckets. From the buckets, they're soon transferred to packing trays in boxes, so the peaches are handled only twice before they're shipped. More traditional harvest methods for peaches have the fruit dropped into large bins in which the layers of fruit create enough pressure that would crush tender, fully ripe fruit. Then they're dumped from bins into larger storage containers where they may be warehoused for a few days before being boxed up for shipment. It takes a pretty firm fruit to withstand that kind of handling, fruit that doesn't mature quite as much on the tree, which can lessen its overall capacity for ripeness. The truly tree-ripe peach is not the norm at the market, but it is definitely worth seeking out.

Jam-Filled Doughnuts

Nothing beats the melt-in-your-mouth taste of homemade doughnuts. They take a bit of time, but aren't difficult to make. The filling in this recipe is a sort of shortcut jam recipe. The fruit mixture is cooked long enough to reduce and thicken, which also concentrates the luscious fruit flavors. The filling is a great opportunity for using fruit combinations, such as plum and cherry or apricot and peach. For an even bigger shortcut, you could use premium store-bought jam that isn't too chunky; freezer jam offers a great fresh fruit flavor, a good option for this recipe.

Plan on enjoying these doughnuts soon after they're made; the light, airy texture of the doughnut diminishes after a few hours.

1½ cups milk	½ teaspoon salt
½ cup sugar	1 egg, lightly beaten
¼ cup unsalted butter, cut into pieces	Vegetable oil, for frying doughnuts
4 cups all-purpose flour	Powdered sugar, for sprinkling
2 teaspoons (1 envelope) active dry yeast	

Jam Filling

10 ounces stone fruit, pitted and coarsely chopped (peaches peeled first, if using)	3 tablespoons freshly squeezed lemon juice
	½ cup sugar

For the jam filling, purée the fruit with the lemon juice in a food processor or blender until quite smooth, scraping down the sides of the bowl once or twice. Put the purée in a small, heavy saucepan and stir in the sugar. Cook over medium-high heat for 5 minutes, stirring often to help the sugar dissolve. Decrease the heat to medium and cook until the mixture is thickened, stirring often, 30 to 45 minutes, depending on the fruit used. To test the "gel," spoon a little bit on a small plate and put it in the freezer for a few minutes to quickly chill, then check its texture; it should hold its shape and be quite thick. Let the jam filling cool completely, then refrigerate until ready to use.

Put the milk in a small saucepan and bring just to a low boil over medium heat. Take the pan from the heat and stir in the sugar and butter until they are dissolved and melted, respectively. Let cool to about 108°F (warm, not hot, to the touch), and then stir in 1 cup of the flour and the yeast. Set this "sponge" aside in a warm place until frothy, about 15 minutes.

Meanwhile, put the remaining flour in a large bowl and stir in the salt, then make a well in the center. Add the yeast sponge to the well along with the egg and stir gently to evenly blend. Use your hand, lightly floured if necessary to avoid sticking, to gently knead the dough against the side of the bowl for a minute or two to form a cohesive dough; you don't want to knead the dough as much as you would for bread or the doughnuts will be heavy. Cover the bowl with a kitchen towel and let sit in a warm place until doubled in bulk, about 1 hour.

Turn the risen dough onto a lightly floured work surface and press it out to a circle about ½ inch thick (shape doesn't matter much but thickness should be even). Using a 3-inch round cutter or glass rim, cut the dough into circles, dipping the cutter in flour as needed to avoid sticking.

Transfer the dough rounds to two lightly floured trays, leaving a couple of inches between the rounds. When you've cut all the rounds you can, gently draw the trimmings together, pressing and pinching together the cut edges to form a solid circle and cut more rounds—you should have about 12 total. (Avoid handling the dough too much, or the doughnuts will not be light and fluffy.) Cover the trays with dish towels and let rise in a warm place until doubled, about 1 hour.

When ready to fry the doughnuts, heat a few inches of vegetable oil in a large, heavy pot, such as a Dutch oven, to 350°F. The oil should come no more than halfway up the sides of the pot. Gently add a few doughnuts to the hot oil and fry until browned and puffed, 3 to 4 minutes, carefully turning them a few times so they brown evenly but lightly. Scoop out the doughnuts with a slotted spoon and drain on paper towels. Continue with the remaining doughnuts, allowing the oil to reheat between batches as needed. Let the doughnuts cool before filling.

To fill the doughnuts, spoon the jam into a pastry bag fitted with a small, plain tip. With the slender end of a wooden spoon or a chopstick, make a hole in the side of a doughnut about to the center of the doughnut. Insert the tip of the pastry bag in the hole and gently squeeze in a tablespoon or so of the jam (don't overfill or you'll have jam oozing back out the hole). Repeat with the remaining doughnuts, arranging them on a serving platter. Sprinkle the tops lightly with powdered sugar and serve.

Makes 12 doughnuts

Lemon-Cherry Tea Bread

This zesty quick bread makes the most of sweet fresh cherries to add flavor, color, and moistness to the lemony batter. Rainier cherries, with their pale flesh, won't bleed into the batter as Bing or other red cherries will, but they also won't offer the vibrant color contrast. Frozen pitted sweet cherries are a good off-season alternative; use about 1½ cups chopped pitted cherries (they don't need to be thawed before stirring into the batter).

1½ cups all-purpose flour	1 tablespoon grated lemon zest
1½ teaspoons baking powder	½ cup milk
¼ teaspoon salt	¾ pound sweet cherries
½ cup unsalted butter, at room temperature	¾ cup chopped walnuts
¾ cup granulated sugar	½ cup powdered sugar
2 eggs	1 tablespoon freshly squeezed lemon juice

Preheat the oven to 350°F. Generously butter a 9-by-5-inch loaf pan.

Sift together the flour, baking powder, and salt onto a piece of waxed paper or into a small bowl. In a medium bowl, cream the butter and sugar with an electric mixer at medium speed until well blended and fluffy. Add the eggs and lemon zest and continue beating until well blended, scraping down the sides a few times. With the motor running at low speed, add the flour mixture alternating with the milk.

Pit and coarsely chop the cherries, then use a rubber spatula to stir the cherries and walnuts evenly into the batter. Spoon the batter into the prepared loaf pan, spreading the top evenly and tapping the pan gently on the counter to help reduce air bubbles in the batter. Bake until the bread is nicely browned and cooked through (a toothpick inserted into the center of the bread should come out clean), about 1 hour. Let cool slightly in the pan set on a wire rack, then turn the bread out onto the rack to cool completely.

Sift the powdered sugar into a small bowl, pressing on any little clumps to break them up, then stir in the lemon juice to make a smooth glaze. When the bread is cool, drizzle the glaze over the bread and let dry. Cut the tea bread into slices and serve.

Makes 8 to 12 servings

Fried Polenta with Plum Compote

When I was growing up, this simple but tasty breakfast was common morning fare in my house. There's no Italian blood (that I know of) running through my family's veins, so the dish was unceremoniously called "fried cornmeal mush," though it was no less delicious. We simply poured warm maple syrup over the hot slices of fried polenta before digging in, but the tart-sweet flavor of this Plum Compote is another tasty foil for the nutty-rich flavor of the polenta. Moderately sweet eating plums are preferable here to the more sugary prune-plums, especially red varieties such as Santa Rosa or Elephant Heart. Crisp bacon would be an ideal accompaniment. Off-season, consider using frozen peach slices or pitted cherries in place of the plums.

The polenta should chill for at least a few hours to assure that it's firm enough to unmold and slice for frying, so plan ahead. You may make the polenta and the compote a day ahead and refrigerate, so you have only to fry, reheat, and serve the next morning.

4 cups water	1 tablespoon grated orange zest
1 teaspoon salt	3 to 4 tablespoons unsalted butter,
1½ cups polenta (coarse cornmeal)	for frying the polenta

Plum Compote

½ cup freshly squeezed orange juice	2 cinnamon sticks
⅓ cup sugar, or to taste	1½ pounds ripe but firm plums
1 teaspoon grated orange zest	

Generously butter a 9-by-5-inch loaf pan.

Put the water and salt in a medium, heavy saucepan and bring to a boil. Slowly stir the cornmeal into the boiling water, then reduce the heat to medium-low and cook, stirring constantly, until the cornmeal is thickened and tender, 8 to 10 minutes. (The polenta will begin to sputter as it thickens, so be sure to use a long-handled wooden spoon.) Add the orange zest and stir to evenly incorporate. Pour the cornmeal into the loaf pan, smoothing the top evenly. Let sit until nearly cool, then cover and refrigerate for at least 3 hours or overnight.

For the plum compote, combine the orange juice, sugar, orange zest, and cinnamon sticks in a medium saucepan. Bring the mixture just to a boil over medium-high heat; then lower the heat to medium and simmer until the liquids have reduced by half, about 10 minutes.

Meanwhile, pit and quarter the plums, then add them to the pan and simmer until tender, stirring occasionally, 10 to 12 minutes longer. Keep warm over low heat while frying the polenta.

Unmold the polenta onto a cutting board and cut it into 12 slices. Heat 2 tablespoons of the butter in a large, heavy skillet, preferably nonstick, over medium heat. When melted, gently swirl the butter to evenly coat the pan and add a few of the polenta slices. Cook until lightly browned and heated through, 3 to 5 minutes per side. Transfer the slices to a heatproof plate and keep warm in a low oven while frying the remaining polenta, adding more butter to the skillet as needed.

To serve, arrange 2 slices of Fried Polenta, slightly overlapping, on each plate. Spoon some of the Plum Compote over and serve right away.

Makes 6 servings

Cinnamon Crêpes with Spiced Cherries

This variation on the simple dessert crêpe is a great eye-opener for a lazy weekend brunch, though it may be served as an equally delicious finish to your evening meal. Thin and delicate crêpes are embellished with the aromatic flavor of cinnamon before enclosing a filling of sweet cherries also accented with cinnamon. Any sweet cherry can be used here.

Frozen pitted cherries or top-quality canned cherries (two 15-ounce cans) may be used in place of fresh fruit off-season. If using canned cherries, use about ¾ cup of the strained liquid in place of the orange juice and add 1 tablespoon grated orange zest to the mixture. Sugar may not be needed, depending on the sweetness of the syrup in which the cherries are canned, so just add sugar to taste.

½ cup freshly squeezed orange juice	½ teaspoon freshly ground or
2 teaspoons cornstarch	grated nutmeg
2 pounds sweet cherries	Pinch salt
⅓ cup granulated sugar	⅔ cup whipping cream
½ teaspoon ground cinnamon	1 to 2 tablespoons powdered sugar

Cinnamon Crêpes

1 cup all-purpose flour	1¼ cups milk
3 tablespoons granulated sugar	2 tablespoons unsalted butter, melted
1½ teaspoons ground cinnamon	and cooled, plus more for cooking
½ teaspoon salt	the crêpes
3 eggs	

For the crêpes, sift together the flour, sugar, cinnamon, and salt into a medium bowl, then make a well in the center. Put the eggs in a small bowl and beat with a fork just to mix, then add the milk and stir to blend. Pour the egg-and-milk mixture into the well in the flour and slowly incorporate the flour just until mixed. It's important not to overmix the batter or the crêpes will be tough rather than tender; a few fine lumps are okay. Add the melted butter and stir just to incorporate. Cover with plastic wrap and refrigerate for 1 to 2 hours before cooking the crêpes.

Stir together 2 tablespoons of the orange juice with the cornstarch in a small bowl (use some of the cherry syrup in place of the orange juice if using canned cherries); set aside. Pit the cherries.

In a medium saucepan, combine the remaining orange juice, sugar, cinnamon, ¼ teaspoon of the nutmeg, and salt. Bring the mixture to a boil over medium-high heat, then reduce the heat immediately, add the cherries, and simmer, stirring occasionally, until the cherries are tender but not mushy, 8 to 10 minutes. Stir the orange juice–cornstarch mixture, then add it to the cherries and stir until the liquid thickens, 2 to 3 minutes. Keep the cherry filling warm over very low heat while you make the crêpes.

Lightly coat an 8-inch crêpe pan or medium nonstick skillet with melted butter and heat it over medium heat. Stir the batter once again to remix. Add a scant ¼ cup of the batter to the pan and quickly but gently swirl the pan so the batter evenly coats the bottom. Cook the crêpe until the top surface turns from shiny to dull and the edges are just beginning to curl, 30 to 60 seconds. Using a small spatula, carefully flip the crêpe and cook on the second side until it is lightly browned, about 1 minute longer. Continue with the remaining crêpes, stacking them one on top of the other. It's very common for the first (and sometimes second) crêpe to be a total failure, so don't think twice about tossing out early crêpes that don't work. You want a total of 8 crêpes in the end.

Whip the cream in a medium bowl with an electric mixer at medium-high speed until it begins to thicken, then add the powdered sugar (to taste) and the remaining ¼ teaspoon of nutmeg. Continue whipping until soft peaks form.

Lay one crêpe on a serving plate with the more attractive side down. Spoon a heaping ¼ cup of the spiced cherries down the center of the crêpe, then fold one long edge over the filling and loosely roll up the crêpe in a cylinder, turning so that the seam is underneath. Repeat with another crêpe alongside the first. Continue with the remaining crêpes and filling, two per serving. Top the crêpes with a dollop of whipped cream and serve right away.

Makes 4 servings

Yogurt Cheese with Poached Fruit and Cinnamon-Sugar Oats

Yogurt cheese isn't real cheese, at least not in a traditional sense. To make it, yogurt is allowed to drain, drawing off the liquid whey, leaving the remaining yogurt firmer and more concentrated in flavor. I much prefer using whole-milk yogurt to lowfat or nonfat in this recipe, because lowfat and nonfat don't have the creamy texture that whole-milk yogurt does. If you use vanilla yogurt, remember that it is generally lightly sweetened; if using plain yogurt you might want to add a bit of honey. You may embellish the cinnamon-sugar oats with a bit of shredded coconut or slivered almonds or both, if you like.

The poached fruit, yogurt cheese, and oats may be prepared a day ahead, so you'll have nothing to do but assemble the dish come breakfast time. Dried and frozen fruit make great substitutions for fresh out of season.

1 large container (4 cups) vanilla or plain yogurt	1 cup rolled oats
2 tablespoons unsalted butter	2 tablespoons sugar
	½ teaspoon ground cinnamon

Poached Fruit

2½ cups water	1 star anise
½ cup sugar	4 ripe but firm apricots
Pared zest from 1 small lemon	3 ripe but firm plums
4 whole cloves	1 ripe but firm nectarine

Line a fine sieve with a double thickness of cheesecloth and set over a medium bowl. Spoon the yogurt into the sieve, cover with plastic wrap, and refrigerate for at least 4 hours or overnight.

For the poached fruit, combine the water, sugar, lemon zest, cloves, and star anise in a medium saucepan over medium-high heat. Bring just to a boil, stirring often to help the sugar dissolve, then reduce the heat to medium-low.

Pit the fruit, cutting the plums and nectarine into ½-inch slices and leaving the apricots in halves. Add the fruit to the poaching liquid and simmer gently until it is just tender but not falling apart, 15 to 20 minutes, depending on the ripeness of the fruit. Take the pan from the heat and let cool; then refrigerate until ready to serve.

Heat the butter in a small skillet over medium heat until melted, then add the oats and stir to evenly coat them in the butter. Sprinkle with the sugar and cinnamon and stir to mix. Cook the oats, stirring constantly, until the sugar has lightly caramelized and the oats are toasty-brown, 5 to 7 minutes. Transfer the oats to a piece of foil and spread them out in an even layer to cool. When fully cooled, store the oats in an airtight container until ready to serve.

To serve, spoon some of the drained yogurt cheese into individual bowls (discard the whey that has drained from the yogurt). Scoop the fruit from its poaching liquid with a slotted spoon and add it to the bowls, distributing the different fruits more or less evenly. Scatter the cinnamon-sugar oats over, drizzle some of the poaching liquid over, and serve right away.

Makes 4 to 6 servings

Pared or Grated? Pared zest of lemon and other citrus fruit isn't exactly the same as grated zest. When grating, you make fine little shavings of zest that will be incorporated into a dish. But for paring, you're simply peeling off large strips of zest (using a vegetable peeler or paring knife) that will infuse a dish with flavor and be removed before serving. For both techniques, try to get just the bright yellow outer layer and avoid the bitter white pith.

Appetizers, Salads, and Side Dishes

Chicken Salad with Tarragon and Plums

This flavorful salad is delicious as is for a lunch dish or on hearty bread for a delectable chicken salad sandwich. You may also spoon it into endive leaves for cocktail-style finger food, but chop the chicken and plums a bit finer so the salad won't be too chunky in that variation. The poaching liquid retains savory flavor and may be strained and saved (a week in the refrigerator, a couple of months if frozen) to use as you would chicken stock.

½ cup loosely packed celery leaves or coarsely chopped celery

2 tarragon sprigs

10 to 12 whole peppercorns

Salt

3 boneless, skinless chicken breasts, about 6 ounces each

8 ounces ripe but firm plums

½ cup finely chopped celery

½ cup mayonnaise, preferably homemade (see page 35)

2 teaspoons minced tarragon

Freshly ground black pepper

1 small head Bibb lettuce, leaves separated, rinsed, and dried

Half-fill a deep skillet with water and add the celery leaves, tarragon sprigs, peppercorns, and a good pinch of salt. Bring just to a boil, then lower the heat to medium and add the chicken breasts (check that the breasts are fully covered with water; add a bit more hot water if needed). Simmer gently until the chicken is just cooked through, about 15 minutes. Cut into the thick part of the breast to check; you should not see any pink flesh. Avoid overcooking the chicken or it will become tough and flavorless.

Transfer the chicken to a plate lined with paper towels and set aside to cool. (If saving the cooking liquid for another use, let cool in the pan, then strain through a sieve lined with wet paper towels and store in a plastic airtight container.)

When the chicken is fully cooled, cut it into about ½-inch dice and put it in a large bowl. Pit and dice the plums and add them to the bowl with the celery, mayonnaise, and minced tarragon. Toss gently to evenly mix, and season the salad to taste with salt and pepper.

Line each plate with some of the lettuce leaves, spoon the chicken salad in the center, and serve right away.

Makes 4 servings

Homemade Mayonnaise

1 egg yolk
2 teaspoons tarragon vinegar or white wine vinegar
¾ cup olive oil (not extra-virgin)
Salt and freshly ground white pepper

In a medium bowl, combine the egg yolk with the vinegar and whisk to blend. Begin adding the olive oil a few drops at a time, whisking constantly, until the yolk begins to turn pale and thicken slightly, showing that an emulsion has begun to form. Continue adding the rest of the oil in a thin, steady stream, whisking constantly. Season to taste with salt and pepper. Alternatively, combine the egg yolk and vinegar in a food processor and pulse to blend. With the blades running, begin adding the oil a few drops at a time until the emulsion begins to form, then continue adding the rest of the oil in a thin, steady stream. Add the salt and pepper to taste and pulse to blend.

Refrigerate the mayonnaise, covered, until ready to serve; it may be made a day or two in advance.

Makes a generous ¾ cup

Bacon and Blue Cheese Salad with Cherry Vinaigrette

For this yummy, rather decadent salad, you may use Rainier or other pale cherries in place of the dark cherries, though you'll miss out on the deep crimson color the dark cherries provide the vinaigrette dressing. Dried cherries are a tasty off-season alternative. Plump about ½ cup dried sweet cherries in warm water, and then drain well. Continue as for the fresh, using half in the dressing and tossing the other half with the salad. When Walla Walla sweet onions aren't available, you may use thinly sliced red onion (which will be hotter) or a handful of sliced green onions in their place.

4 thick slices bacon, cut into
  ½-inch pieces
8 ounces mixed salad greens (baby
  spinach, arugula, red leaf lettuce,
frisée, romaine), rinsed, tough stems
  removed, and dried
½ small Walla Walla sweet onion,
  thinly sliced
½ cup crumbled Oregon blue cheese

Cherry Vinaigrette

¾ pound Bing or other
  dark sweet cherries
¼ cup white wine vinegar
⅓ cup olive oil
Salt and freshly ground black pepper

For the cherry vinaigrette, pit and halve the cherries and set aside half of them to toss with the salad later. Put the remaining cherries in a food processor or blender with the vinegar and purée until smooth. Add the olive oil and salt and pepper to taste, and purée for another few seconds. Transfer the vinaigrette to a small bowl and set aside. (A blender will purée the cherries more finely than a food processor; if using the latter, you may want to strain out the bits of cherry skin after processing, pressing on the solids with the back of a rubber spatula to extract as much juice as possible.)

Fry the bacon pieces in a small skillet over medium-high heat until browned and crisp, stirring occasionally, about 5 minutes. Scoop them onto paper towels to drain; set aside to cool.

Chukar Cherries

After just a few years of growing cherries in the Yakima Valley of Washington State, Pam Auld was inspired to find a way to do more with the beautiful and luscious sweet fruit than just selling them for the brief fresh summer market. So in 1988, Auld began drying her cherries in her own distinctive way, and today she has a thriving business selling dried fruits, confections, jams, and other fruit products throughout the Northwest and beyond.

The Chukar line of products includes many fruits—blueberries from the Olympia area, cranberries from southwest Washington, and strawberries from across the Northwest—but cherries still reign, relished by chefs, candy makers, and consumers near and far. Chukar cherries are also popular gift items, both with visiting tourists as an edible souvenir (they have a retail shop in the Pike Place Market) and with locals wanting to share a taste of home when they travel. More than a few times, I have tucked bags of Chukar cherries into my luggage for hostess gifts when traveling to Europe: nonperishable, nonbreakable, and thoroughly delicious.

Many dried fruits are preserved with sulfites or added sugar to prolong their shelf life and hold their color. Chukar products have no preservatives at all, the secret coming from drying fruit that is at its maximum ripeness. Fruit dried when it has a full complement of natural sugars will preserve its color and flavor naturally for many months, up to 18 months or more in the case of Chukar's sweet cherries.

There is a rough five-to-one ratio for dried fruits: it takes about five pounds of fresh fruit to produce one pound of dried. If you've ever looked at a package of dried fruit and been surprised by the cost, this is why. But the fruit is also concentrated and a little goes a long way. One of Auld's favorite uses for dried cherries is in a simple savory sauce to serve with sautéed chicken or pork: Take a good bottle of Northwest red wine, throw in a small handful of dried cherries, and boil until reduced by half, then add a tablespoon of butter and pinch of sugar. Season with salt and pepper, maybe a pinch of fresh herbs, and voilà.

This Prosser-based company is named for a game bird, the chukar, which flourishes in the Yakima Valley. It is so prominent that the National Chukar Trials for bird dogs is held in the Prosser area each spring. The distinctive head of this bird graces the logo of Chukar products, further emphasizing their roots in the region. All Chukar products are available at www.chukar.com.

Put the salad greens in a salad bowl or other large bowl and scatter the onion and bacon over the top. Rewhisk the Cherry Vinaigrette to blend, and taste for seasoning, adding a bit more salt or pepper if needed. Drizzle the vinaigrette over the salad, tossing to mix gently and evenly. Arrange the salad on 4 individual plates and sprinkle the blue cheese and remaining cherries evenly over each portion. Serve right away.

Makes 4 servings

Apricot Couscous Salad

This tasty salad may be served as a light main course or a vegetarian entrée (adding a few more vegetables, if you like, to make it more substantial). Or it makes a perfect accompaniment to roasted chicken, Peach-and-Curry-Glazed Cornish Hens (page 52) or Grilled Salmon with Cardamom-Peach Chutney (page 47).

Using both fresh and dried apricots in this salad produces a nice blend of the concentrated sweetness from dried fruit plus aromatic flavor from fresh apricots. You may also use just one or the other depending on your taste and the season.

½ cup sliced almonds
6 tablespoons olive oil
½ onion, finely chopped
1 teaspoon ground cumin
½ teaspoon turmeric
¼ teaspoon freshly ground
   or grated nutmeg
¼ teaspoon ground ginger
Salt and freshly ground black pepper
3 cups chicken or vegetable stock

1 box (10 ounces, about 1⅔ cups)
   instant couscous
4 ounces dried apricots, chopped
8 ounces fresh apricots
1½ cups finely diced zucchini
1 can (15½ ounces) chickpeas,
   rinsed and well drained
¼ cup finely chopped flat-leaf
   (Italian) parsley
⅓ cup freshly squeezed lemon juice,
   more to taste

Preheat the oven to 350°F.

Scatter the almonds in a baking pan and toast until lightly browned and aromatic, about 5 minutes, gently shaking the pan once or twice to help the nuts toast evenly. Set aside.

Heat 2 tablespoons of the olive oil in a large saucepan over medium heat. Add the onion and cook, stirring, until tender and aromatic, 3 to 5 minutes. Stir in the cumin, turmeric, nutmeg, and ginger with a generous pinch of salt and pepper and cook, stirring, for 1 minute longer. Add the stock and bring just to a boil. Slowly add the couscous, stirring constantly, then take the pan from the heat and stir in the dried apricot pieces. Cover the pan and set aside for 15 minutes. Transfer the couscous to a large bowl and stir to fluff the grains; let cool, stirring occasionally.

When the couscous is cooled, pit and finely chop the fresh apricots and add them to the couscous along with the zucchini, chickpeas, and parsley, stirring to mix evenly. Combine the lemon juice with the remaining 4 tablespoons of the olive oil in a small bowl and beat with a fork to mix, then pour over the couscous salad, tossing to coat evenly. Taste the salad for seasoning, adding more lemon juice, salt, or pepper to taste. The salad may be served right away, though it will have more flavor if refrigerated for at least a few hours before serving.

Spoon the salad onto 8 individual plates, sprinkle with the toasted almonds, and serve.

Makes 8 servings

Aged Cougar Gold with Apricot Paste

This intriguing recipe is a Northwest take on the classic Spanish combination of manchego cheese (an aged sheep's milk cheese from the Mancha region of Spain) with quince paste. The rich, nutty character of aged Cougar Gold cheese (see page 41) pairs wonderfully with toasted almonds and the sweet-tart flavor of apricot paste. Quince have loads of pectin, so the paste of that fruit sets up naturally. Apricots, alas, have less pectin, and thus the addition of pectin helps set the paste. The puréed fruit is cooked with sugar and lemon juice (both of which are critical elements to promote setting, so don't be tempted to omit either), producing a concentrated apricot flavor. Off-season, dried apricots could be used: Plump 4 ounces of dried apricots in warm water and purée with 4 to 5 tablespoons of their soaking liquid. The purée will take just 10 to 15 minutes to cook.

Rather than serving this dish as an appetizer, you could serve it after dinner—the ideal dessert for cheese lovers and those who don't have much of a sweet tooth.

1 pound apricots

½ cup sugar

3 tablespoons freshly squeezed lemon juice

1 package powdered pectin

1 cup whole blanched almonds

2 teaspoons olive oil

½ teaspoon coarse salt

12 ounces aged Cougar Gold cheese or other sharp cheese

Halve and pit the apricots and purée them in a food processor until very smooth, scraping down the sides of the food processor bowl as needed. Put the apricot purée in a small saucepan with the sugar and lemon juice. Bring the mixture to a boil over medium-high heat, stirring often, then reduce the heat to medium-low and cook until the purée is slightly thickened and deepens in color somewhat, 20 to 25 minutes, stirring often. Be careful to avoid scorching; reduce the heat or take the pan from the heat for a few moments if the purée seems to be sticking. Use a heat-proof spatula to fully scrape the purée from the bottom of the pan as you stir.

Little by little, sprinkle the pectin over the fruit, stirring constantly to help it dissolve. When all the pectin has been stirred in, increase the heat to medium-high and cook for 1 minute longer, stirring constantly. Transfer the paste to an 8-inch square pan, spreading it out evenly. Let cool completely, then cover the pan and refrigerate until fully set, 1 to 2 hours. The paste may be made up to a week in advance and refrigerated, covered.

Preheat the oven to 350°F.

Put the almonds in a small baking dish, drizzle with the olive oil, and toss to evenly coat. Toast the almonds until they are nutty smelling and deep golden brown, 12 to 15 minutes, stirring the nuts a few times so they toast evenly. Take the pan from the oven, sprinkle with salt, and toss to coat. The nuts may be toasted a day ahead and stored in an airtight container.

To serve, cut the cheese into ½-inch-thick slices or into individual wedges and put to one side of each plate. Cut the apricot paste into 2-inch squares or diamonds and set 2 or 3 pieces opposite the cheese, with a small pile of the toasted almonds alongside.

Makes 6 to 8 servings

Cougar Gold Cheese

There is no mistaking Cougar Gold cheese: it's one of the few, if not the only, cheeses sold in a can. The cheddar-style cheese was first created on the campus of Washington State University in Pullman in the 1940s and is still made there today. Originally, this canned cheese was an experiment with the new metal can packaging that was making waves in the food world early in the twentieth century. But cheese didn't naturally take well to canning, because it produces gases as it ages, thus bulging the cans and causing safety complications and spoilage hazards.

Enter WSU food scientist Dr. N. S. Golding, who participated in research—cosponsored by the U.S. government and the American Can Company— to develop cheese that would not emit gas while aging, thus a better candidate for canning. The resulting cheese was named in honor of the school's mascot—the cougar—and Dr. Golding: Cougar Gold was born.

About 275,000 pounds of the cheese was made in one recent year, packed into cans holding 30 ounces each. The cheese is aged at least one year before being sold, so it has an already-distinctive flavor at the time of purchase. But if you put that can on a shelf of your refrigerator and age it for another six months or a year, the flavor will develop even more. It's a great treat, if you're patient! The delicious cheese (along with other WSU Creamery cheeses, including their Jack-style Viking cheese) is just a phone call away for door-to-door delivery (year-round, except during hot summer months): 800-457-5442.

Seared Scallops with Caramelized Nectarines

This simple, scrumptious dish proves the cook's adage that when you've got great ingredients, the best thing to do with them is as little as possible. Buy the best scallops you can—large sea scallops that are "dry pack" (ask the fishmonger), which means that they will not have been treated with chemicals to keep them plumped up with water (which you're paying for, and which seeps out during cooking).

For a total splurge, you could replace the scallops with slices of foie gras, that delectable liver from fatted geese or ducks. The technique would be virtually the same as for scallops, omitting the oil and making certain to fully preheat the pan before adding the sliced foie gras so that the surface quickly sears and as little of the fat as possible melts into the pan.

2 tablespoons sugar	12 large sea scallops (about 1 pound)
1 ripe but firm nectarine	Salt and freshly ground black pepper
3 tablespoons canola oil	2 tablespoons brandy (optional)

Put the sugar on a small plate. Pit the nectarine and cut it into eighths. Lightly dip the cut edges of each nectarine piece in the sugar. Heat 1 tablespoon of the oil in a small skillet, preferably nonstick, over medium heat. Add the nectarine pieces, cut-side down, and cook until the sugar is lightly caramelized and the nectarine is nearly tender through, 8 to 10 minutes total, turning the pieces a few times.

While the nectarines are cooking, heat the remaining 2 tablespoons of oil in a medium skillet, preferably nonstick, over medium-high heat. Season the scallops with salt and pepper. When the oil is just beginning to smoke, carefully add the scallops and cook until well browned, 1 to 2 minutes. Turn the scallops and continue cooking until browned on the second side and there's a bit of translucence left in the center of the scallops, about 1 minute. (They'll continue to cook in the residual heat once taken from the pan.)

Arrange the scallops on warmed plates with the nectarine pieces alongside. For an optional final flourish, add the brandy to the skillet that held the caramelized nectarines and carefully light it with a long match. Gently toss the skillet over medium heat until the flames die away and drizzle these pan juices around both. Serve right away.

Makes 4 servings

Beef and Apricot Saté

Borrowing from the Indonesian style of grilled kebabs, in this recipe marinated chunks of beef are threaded onto skewers with pieces of fragrant fresh apricot, making a luscious sweet-savory blend to serve as an appetizer for a summer grilling party. Or, for a main course, prepare a dozen satés on longer skewers and serve 3 per serving over a bed of steamed jasmine rice with sautéed vegetables alongside. You may use lamb instead of beef, if you like.

¼ cup olive oil
1 tablespoon freshly squeezed
   lemon juice
2 teaspoons minced garlic
2 teaspoons minced or grated ginger
1 teaspoon ground cumin

¼ teaspoon cayenne pepper
¼ teaspoon salt
Big pinch freshly ground black pepper
6 ripe but firm apricots
2 pounds beef sirloin or tenderloin,
   cut into ¾-inch pieces

Preheat an outdoor grill. Soak 24 bamboo skewers (6 inches long) in cold water.

In a medium bowl, combine the olive oil, lemon juice, garlic, ginger, cumin, cayenne, salt, and pepper. Stir to mix. Pit and quarter the apricots, then add them to the marinade and toss quickly. Scoop them out with a slotted spoon and set aside on a plate. Add the beef to the marinade, tossing to coat well. Let sit until the grill is ready. (The beef can be prepared a couple of hours in advance, though it should be refrigerated if more than 30 minutes before cooking or if your kitchen is quite warm.)

Drain the soaked skewers. Thread a piece of beef onto one skewer. Follow with a piece of apricot, threading it on lengthwise, and finish with another piece of beef. Continue with the remaining beef and apricots.

When the grill is heated, lightly brush the grill grate with oil and grill the skewers until the beef is browned and medium-rare, about 2 minutes per side (or longer, to suit your taste). Arrange the skewers on a serving platter and serve right away.

Makes 6 to 8 servings

Silky Chicken Liver Pâté with Brandied Cherries

This luxurious pâté is oh so easy to make. Using some of the liquid from brandy-soaked cherries adds good flavor, but it's still best to add some brandy, which brings a welcome bite to contrast with the richness of the livers. Instead of forming the pâté in individual ramekins, you could form it in a small loaf pan to serve on a buffet table. You may use ⅓ cup coarsely chopped dried cherries in place of the fresh: combine them with the ½ cup brandy and the ½ cup hot water to plump them.

⅓ pound Bing or other dark sweet
  cherries
½ cup plus 2 tablespoons brandy
1 pound chicken livers
¾ cup unsalted butter,
  at room temperature

¾ cup finely chopped shallot or onion
1 tablespoon minced garlic
Salt and freshly ground black pepper
½ teaspoon minced thyme
1 small baguette, thinly sliced

Pit and coarsely chop the fresh cherries and combine them with ½ cup of the brandy in a small bowl and toss to mix. Set aside while preparing the pâté, stirring occasionally.

Use a small knife to cut away the membrane from the chicken livers. Heat 2 tablespoons of the butter in a medium skillet over medium heat. Add the shallot and garlic and cook, stirring, until tender and aromatic, 2 to 3 minutes. Add the chicken livers with a good pinch of salt and pepper and cook, stirring often, until the livers are evenly browned and cooked through (cut into a few pieces; there should be no pink left in the center), 10 to 12 minutes. Set the skillet aside to let the livers cool for 10 to 15 minutes.

Transfer the livers to a food processor, being careful to scrape all the shallot and other flavorful bits from the skillet. Add the remaining butter, ½ cup of the cherry-soaking liquid, the remaining 2 tablespoons of brandy, and thyme and process until very smooth, scraping down the sides of the processor bowl as needed. Transfer the purée to a medium bowl and fold in the brandied cherries.

Taste the mixture for seasoning, adding salt and pepper as needed. Spoon into six ½-cup ramekins or other small dishes, smoothing the top, and cover with plastic wrap. Refrigerate until well chilled and set, at least 2 hours.

To serve, set the ramekins on individual plates, arrange bread slices alongside, and serve.

Makes 6 servings

Main Courses

Cherry-Roasted Leg of Lamb with Spicy Cherry Salsa

Roasted leg of lamb is one of life's simplest and most delicious treats, as welcome for a special occasion as for Sunday supper. Garlic, the common lamb partner, isn't forgotten in this recipe, though cherries are puréed with the garlic to make a luscious crust that adds a touch of tangy sweetness to the meat. A simple salsa of sweet cherries and onions gets some zip from jalapeño, a delicious complement to the lamb. The salsa is also tasty with grilled chicken or roasted pork, or even just a basket of chips.

8 ounces Bing or other dark
    sweet cherries
2 tablespoons olive oil
4 cloves garlic, chopped

1 leg of lamb, bone-in (5 to 6 pounds)
    or boned (4 to 5 pounds)
Salt and freshly ground black pepper

Cherry Salsa

8 ounces Bing or other dark
    sweet cherries
½ cup finely chopped yellow onion
¼ cup chopped green onion

2 tablespoons minced cilantro
2 tablespoons freshly squeezed
    lime juice
1 tablespoon minced jalapeño chile

Preheat the oven to 350°F.

Pit and coarsely chop the cherries. Purée them in a food processor or blender with the olive oil and garlic until smooth. Generously season the lamb on all sides with salt and pepper. For a bone-in leg, set it in a roasting pan and spread the cherry paste evenly all over the surface of the lamb. If using a boned leg, lay it out flat on the work surface, boned-side up, and spread with about half of the cherry paste. Roll up the meat, secure it with a few pieces of kitchen string, and rub the surface with the remaining cherry paste.

Roast the lamb until a meat thermometer inserted in the center reads 135°F for medium-rare, 140°F for medium, about 1¼ hours (1 hour for a boned leg of lamb).

While the lamb is roasting, make the cherry salsa. Pit and finely chop the cherries and put them in a medium bowl with the yellow onion, green onion, cilantro, lime juice, and jalapeño. Stir to evenly mix, and season the salsa to taste with salt and pepper. Refrigerate until ready to serve.

When the lamb leg is cooked to the appropriate temperature for your taste, take the pan from the oven, cover it with foil, and let sit for 10 minutes. This resting time allows the juices in the meat to redistribute evenly and completes the cooking of the meat, which will continue with residual heat.

Transfer the leg to a carving board and cut it into about ½-inch slices, working at a slight angle going from the narrow shank end toward the broader end of the leg. When you get to the bone, turn the leg slightly and continue slicing. If using boned lamb, simply discard the strings and cut it into slices. Arrange the lamb slices on a warmed serving platter or individual plates and spoon the cherry salsa alongside.

Makes 6 to 8 servings

Grilled Salmon with Cardamom-Peach Chutney

Salmon seems to be at its best when grilled. There's something magical about that melding of the fish's own flavor and rich oils with the high heat and smoky elements that come from outdoor cooking. But the salmon may be broiled or pan-fried if you prefer, or if the weather doesn't allow for outdoor cooking.

Cardamom is one of my favorite spices, with a complex perfumy, slightly citrusy flavor that I like very much with seafood. Green and white cardamom pods are generally available in well-stocked grocery stores or in spice markets. The two are essentially the same; the latter pods have simply been bleached. Brown cardamom is less common and not a true cardamom; it doesn't make a good substitute for the green or white pods. If unable to find cardamom pods, use ground cardamom (about 1 teaspoon), though it won't be as aromatic as freshly ground cardamom.

4 salmon steaks or fillet pieces, 6 to 8 ounces each
1 tablespoon olive oil

Salt and freshly ground black pepper
2 tablespoons chopped cilantro

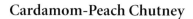

Cardamom-Peach Chutney

14 green or white cardamom pods
1½ teaspoons coriander seeds
½ teaspoon cumin seeds
2 large ripe but firm peaches
2 tablespoons olive oil

1 cup finely chopped onion
1 tablespoon minced ginger
¼ cup white vinegar
Pinch dried red pepper flakes
Salt

For the cardamom-peach chutney, combine 8 of the cardamom pods with the coriander seeds and cumin seeds in a small, dry skillet and toast them over medium heat until lightly browned and aromatic, 2 to 3 minutes. Transfer the spices to a spice grinder or a mortar and pestle and finely grind or crush them (the cardamom pods that enclose the seeds are flavorless and are perfectly okay in the spice blend). Set the spices aside. Peel and pit the peaches, then cut them into ½-inch dice.

Heat the oil in a medium skillet over medium heat. Add the onion and ginger and cook, stirring, until fragrant and the onion is beginning to soften, 3 to 5 minutes. Sprinkle the spices over and stir to evenly coat the onion. Add the peaches with the vinegar, red pepper flakes, and remaining 6 cardamom pods.

Reduce the heat to medium-low and cook, stirring occasionally, until the peaches are tender and the chutney is thick and aromatic, 25 to 30 minutes. Don't stir the chutney so much that the peaches become a purée; the pieces should hold their shape somewhat. Season the chutney to taste with salt and set aside to cool. The chutney may be made a few days in advance and refrigerated, but let it come to room temperature before serving.

Preheat an outdoor grill.

Rub the salmon pieces with the oil and season with salt and pepper. Lightly brush the grill grate with oil, set the salmon on the grill (flesh-side down first, if using fillet pieces), and cook until just a touch of translucent pink remains in the center, about 3 to 4 minutes per side, depending on the thickness of the fish (or longer, to suit your taste). Set the salmon on 4 individual warmed plates, spoon some of the cardamom-peach chutney alongside, and sprinkle the cilantro over all. Serve right away.

Makes 4 servings

Plank-Roasted Halibut and Nectarines with Nectarine Butter

Fresh halibut truly shines in this recipe, but when it is not in season, feel free to use whatever fresh fish looks best, such as sturgeon, cod, or salmon. Choose thicker fillet portions of fish, which will cook more slowly than thin fillets, allowing a maximum of woody aroma and flavor to penetrate the fish as it cooks. The Nectarine Butter makes more than is needed for this recipe, but extra will keep well in the freezer. You may slice off portions to set atop just-grilled fish or toss it with sautéed scallops or shrimp.

This recipe works best with fresh fruit (you could use peaches in place of the nectarines, if you like), though thawed frozen fruit that has been well drained to remove excess water may also be used.

2 teaspoons chopped flat-leaf (Italian)
    parsley, plus 4 to 5 sprigs
1 teaspoon chopped thyme,
    plus 4 to 5 sprigs
½ teaspoon minced rosemary

1 tablespoon olive oil
4 halibut fillet pieces, 6 to 8 ounces
    each, or 1½ pounds halibut cheeks
2 ripe but firm nectarines

Nectarine Butter

½ small nectarine
6 tablespoons unsalted butter,
    at room temperature

1 teaspoon minced flat-leaf
    (Italian) parsley
Salt and freshly ground black pepper

For the nectarine butter, chop the nectarine and put it in a food processor with the butter and parsley. Pulse to evenly blend, scraping down the sides as needed. Add a good pinch of salt and pepper and pulse again. Transfer the butter to a piece of waxed paper or plastic wrap about 1 foot long, spooning it lengthwise down the center to a couple of inches from either end. Roll the butter up into a cylinder, twisting the ends of the paper to form a solid roll. Refrigerate until ready to serve.

Preheat the oven to 375°F.

In a small bowl, combine the chopped parsley, chopped thyme, and rosemary with a good pinch of salt and pepper; stir to mix, and then stir in the olive oil. Rub the herb mixture evenly over the fish with your fingers and set the halibut pieces on the baking plank (flesh-side down, if using fillet pieces). Arrange the parsley and thyme sprigs around the fish.

Pit and quarter the nectarines and set the pieces around the fish, on top of the herbs. Bake the halibut and nectarines until the fish is nearly opaque through the thickest part, 20 to 25 minutes, depending on the thickness of the fish, turning the halibut pieces halfway through. (Cooking on wood is a slower process than on traditional baking dishes; if cooking in a regular baking dish, 15 to 20 minutes should be enough time.)

Transfer the halibut to 4 individual plates and set a couple nectarine pieces alongside. Cut 4 slices of nectarine butter, about ½ inch thick, and set them on top of the halibut. Serve right away.

Makes 4 servings

Chicken Sauté with Plums

The slight tang that plums offer makes a perfect match for chicken in this easy preparation. Red plums or other light-skinned plums are best, as dark plums will bleed into the sauce, giving it a murky color. The recipe is equally tasty with pitted dried plums (prunes) as well, scattering about 6 ounces of them over the chicken pieces when they are returned to the pan. Simple boiled new potatoes or mashed russets are ideal alongside.

½ cup all-purpose flour	½ cup chicken broth
Salt and freshly ground black pepper	½ cup dry white wine
1 whole chicken (3½ to 4 pounds), cut into 8 pieces	2 teaspoons minced thyme
	1 teaspoon minced rosemary
2 tablespoons vegetable oil	1½ pounds plums
2 tablespoons unsalted butter	2 tablespoons chopped flat-leaf
1 large onion, sliced	(Italian) parsley

Combine the flour with a generous pinch of salt and pepper on a plate and stir to mix. Coat the chicken pieces well with flour, patting to remove the excess.

Heat the oil and butter in a sauté pan or large, heavy skillet over medium-high heat. When hot, add the chicken pieces and cook until well browned on all sides, 5 to 7 minutes

Plank Cooking

Cooking with wood smoke is one of the most distinctive traditions of the Pacific Northwest, infusing wood aroma and flavor to foods. The tradition goes back to the local Native tribes who cooked salmon over open pits of alderwood fires. For the home cook, a more accommodating variation of plank cooking can be achieved in the oven or on the grill.

Among Northwest chefs, John Howie has likely worked the most to perfect contemporary plank cooking techniques. His study of this method started while developing a distinctly Northwest–Pacific Island menu for Palisade Restaurant in Seattle, where he was chef for ten years. "We wanted a menu that was more 'Northwest' than simply doing the same Pacific Rim–style foods popular in the city," Howie says. And they decided there was almost nothing more Northwest than cooking with alder or cedar wood.

One of the key benefits of plank cooking goes beyond infusing flavorful wood essence: the wood moderates the heat of cooking and keeps the food moist. For that reason, wood plank cooking is especially well suited to seafood. Another of chef Howie's favorite choices for the plank is pork chops, since they're so lean and easy to overcook. Because you don't need to add oil or butter to avoid sticking, plank cooking is a great low-fat option as well. To top it all off, the woody perfume permeates the kitchen for a pleasant aromatherapy session while you cook.

There are two types of planks for cooking. Oven planks are thick and sturdy, often with bolts through their width to prevent warping and a grooved edge to keep cooking liquids from dripping. These planks may be used again and again over many years. Planks moderate the oven's heat, so cooking times on a plank will typically be about 25 percent longer than with traditional baking techniques.

Barbecue planks are thinner, simpler planks intended for one-time use on your outdoor grill. The plank is first soaked in water, then topped with the fish or other food and set on the grill grate. The plank protects the food from direct contact with heat, while giving off flavor-filled steam to keep the food moist. But because of the plank's direct contact with the intense heat of the grill, it typically chars heavily and is good only for a single use.

Howie is such a big fan of plank cooking that he started his own company selling both oven and barbecue planks. That's in addition to his "day job" as chef-owner of Seastar Restaurant & Raw Bar in Bellevue, Washington. If you want to learn more, or perhaps order yourself a plank, check out www.plankcooking.com.

total. Set the chicken aside on a plate and add the onion to the skillet. Reduce the heat to medium and cook just until tender, about 5 minutes. Stir in the chicken broth and wine, followed by the thyme and rosemary, with another pinch of salt and pepper. Reduce the heat to medium-low and return the chicken pieces to the skillet, nestling them into the onion mixture. Cover the pan and simmer gently for 15 minutes.

Meanwhile, halve and pit the plums. Scatter the plum halves over the chicken, cover the pan again, and continue cooking until the chicken is cooked through (cut into a couple pieces to check that there is no more pink) and the plums are tender, about 15 minutes longer.

Arrange the chicken pieces on 4 individual plates, pouring the sauce over and distributing the plum pieces evenly among the plates. (If the sauce is quite thin, you can boil it down for a minute or two after taking the chicken from the pan.) Scatter the parsley over the chicken and serve right away.

Makes 4 servings

Peach-and-Curry-Glazed Cornish Hens

Cornish hens are among my favorite candidates for outdoor grilling. They are easier to manage than chicken and turkey (which take some heat-management practice), and the smoky heat gives the birds a beautiful golden hue that is enhanced by an aromatic glaze of peaches and curry powder. Don't fret when grilling season's over, though, because these birds are also tasty roasted in the oven. Cornish hens (sometimes called rock hens or game hens) are often sold frozen solid, so plan ahead and allow a day or more for the birds to thaw in the refrigerator—they need to be thawed fully before cooking.

Couscous is a great side dish for this flavorful entrée, perhaps the Apricot Couscous Salad (page 38). Another tasty accompaniment if you're grilling is simple grilled peaches: just brush the cut sides of 2 halved, pitted peaches and set them cut-side down on the outer edge of the grill a few minutes before the birds are done.

1 large peach	½ teaspoon salt
2 tablespoons unsalted butter	1 cup alderwood or
½ cup chopped onion	hickory chips (optional)
1 tablespoon curry powder	2 Cornish game hens, about
1 teaspoon sugar	1½ pounds each

Peel, pit, and finely chop the peach and set aside. Heat the butter in a small skillet over medium heat. Add the onion and sauté, stirring occasionally, until tender and fragrant, 2 to 3 minutes. Add the curry powder and cook for 1 to 2 minutes, stirring to evenly coat the onions and to bring out the spice flavor. Add the peach, sugar, and salt and cook until the fruit is quite tender, 8 to 10 minutes. Purée the peach glaze in a food processor (a miniprocessor works best) or blender, then transfer to a bowl and set aside to cool. The glaze can be made up to 2 days in advance and refrigerated, covered.

Preheat an outdoor grill for indirect heat (if using coals) or medium heat (if using gas). Soak the wood chips in a pan of cold water, if using.

Discard the innards from the cavity of the Cornish hens, rinse them inside and out under cold running water, and pat dry with paper towels. Using kitchen string, tie together the leg ends of both birds. Also tie a piece of string around the body about halfway up the breast, so that the string holds down the wing tips. Set the hens on a plate and brush them liberally all over the surface with the peach-curry glaze (if the hens aren't well dried the glaze will have trouble sticking, so you might want to pat the birds dry one last time before brushing).

Drain the wood chips well, if using, and scatter them over the coals (or according to manufacturer's instructions for your gas grill). Lightly brush the grill grate with oil and arrange the hens breast-side up in the center, if using coals, above the area where there are no coals. Cover the grill and cook until the juices run clear when you pierce the thigh with a sharp knife, 45 minutes to 1 hour. Brush the hens with glaze a few times during cooking. Alternatively, roast the hens in a 400°F oven for 1 to 1¼ hours.

When the hens are cooked, transfer them to a cutting board. Using poultry shears or a heavy, sharp knife, cut off and discard the trussing strings. Cut each bird along either side of the backbone (discarding the bone) and halve the birds down the center of the breast. Arrange the hen halves on individual plates and serve right away.

Makes 4 servings

Lamb Burgers with Arugula and Nectarine Catsup

Though we Americans claim ownership of catsup—the smooth, red condiment that is one of our iconic contributions to world cuisine—it has roots that go as far as Malaysia, where *kechap* is a sauce based on fish. Older American cookbooks include a surprising array of catsup recipes, such as the cucumber and apricot versions in *Clever Cooking*, dating back to 1903, and mushroom catsup in my 1946 copy of *The American Woman's Cook Book*. So this recipe for nectarine catsup isn't as novel an idea as you might have thought. The primary ingredients of fruit, vinegar, onion, chiles, sugar, and spices echo those of chutney, which reflects the East Asian roots of this slightly sweet, slightly tangy condiment. Extra nectarine catsup can be delicious with grilled shrimp or as a unique dip for fried calamari.

2 pounds ground lamb	4 small kaiser rolls or hamburger buns
½ cup minced onion	2 ounces arugula, rinsed and dried,
Salt and freshly ground black pepper	tough stems removed

Nectarine Catsup

2 large nectarines	1 tablespoon minced jalapeño chile
2 tablespoons vegetable oil	1 teaspoon salt
½ cup minced onion	¼ teaspoon powdered ginger
1 tablespoon minced garlic	⅛ teaspoon freshly grated nutmeg
½ cup white wine vinegar	Pinch cinnamon
¼ cup packed light brown sugar	

For the nectarine catsup, peel, pit, and coarsely chop the nectarines, then purée them in a food processor; set aside.

Heat the oil in a medium, heavy skillet over medium heat. Add the onion and garlic and cook, stirring occasionally, until tender and aromatic, 3 to 5 minutes. Add the nectarine purée, vinegar, brown sugar, jalapeño, salt, ginger, nutmeg, and cinnamon. Cook over medium-low heat until thick and flavorful, stirring often, about 1 hour. Taste the catsup for seasoning, adding more salt or spice to taste. Let cool, then refrigerate until ready to serve.

Preheat an outdoor grill. Combine the ground lamb and onion with a good pinch of salt and pepper in a medium bowl and thoroughly mix (your clean hands are the best tools for this!). Form the lamb into 4 patties about 4½ inches across. When the grill is heated, lightly brush the grill grate with oil, and grill the burgers until just a touch of pink remains in the center, 3 to 5 minutes per side. While the burgers are cooking, you may lightly toast the rolls or buns at the outer edge of the grill, if you like.

To serve, place the lamb patties on the bottom half of each roll and top with a generous spoonful of the nectarine catsup. Arrange the arugula leaves over the burgers, top with the remaining roll halves, and serve right away.

Makes 4 servings

Spareribs with Plum Barbecue Sauce

Who doesn't love finger-licking-good barbecued spareribs? Most any kind of plum may be used for the barbecue sauce in this recipe. Color won't matter, since the fruit is peeled and then blended with dark molasses, tomato paste, and other ingredients. The plums contribute a subtle fruity sweetness and moisture to the barbecue sauce.

If you like, you may add a smoky element to these ribs, scattering soaked wood chips (such as hickory or mesquite) over the coals or otherwise using chips according to your grill manufacturer's instructions.

2 teaspoons ground cumin
2 teaspoons salt

1 teaspoon freshly ground
    black pepper
5 to 6 pounds pork spareribs

Plum Barbecue Sauce

1½ pounds plums

3 tablespoons vegetable oil

1 cup finely chopped onion

2 tablespoons minced garlic

¼ cup molasses

¼ cup tomato paste

¼ cup packed dark brown sugar

¼ cup red wine vinegar

1 teaspoon salt

½ teaspoon freshly ground
    black pepper

In a small dish, combine the cumin, salt, and pepper and stir to mix. Sprinkle the spice mixture evenly over the spareribs, rubbing it well into the surface of the meat. Put the ribs in a shallow dish and refrigerate for at least 2 hours and up to 8 hours.

For the plum barbecue sauce, bring a medium pan of water to a boil. Score a small **X** on the bottom of each plum, add them to the boiling water, and boil until the plum skin begins to split, 15 to 30 seconds. Drain the plums and let cool. Peel away the skin, pit the plums, and coarsely chop them.

Heat the oil in a medium, heavy saucepan over medium heat. Add the onion and garlic and cook, stirring often, until tender and aromatic, 3 to 5 minutes. Add the plums and cook until the plums are tender and begin falling apart, 5 to 7 minutes, stirring occasionally. Stir in the molasses, tomato paste, brown sugar, and vinegar, reduce the heat to medium-low, and cook until the sauce is very thick, about 45 minutes. As the sauce cooks, smash any chunks of plum against the side of the pan so the sauce will be nearly smooth.

Preheat an outdoor grill for indirect heat if using charcoal or for medium heat for a gas grill. When the grill is heated, lightly brush the grill grate with oil. Brush some of the barbecue sauce on both sides of the ribs and set them on the grill, cover, and cook until very tender, about 2 hours. Turn the ribs every 30 minutes or so, brushing on more of the barbecue sauce each time. When the ribs are cooked through and tender (twist one of the rib bones to check that it gives), remove them to a cutting board, cut between the ribs, and arrange them on a platter. Serve right away.

Makes 8 servings

Farmers Markets

While some grocery stores in the Northwest go out of their way to bring in the best quality and variety of seasonal foods that they can, I still feel that the ultimate urban resource for fruit lovers is regional farmers markets, one of the best trends to hit the Northwest. Each year, a growing number of farmers and consumers come together to help bridge that gap between the city dweller and the dedicated people who work so hard to bring us fresh—often organic—food. The benefits are many: you'll buy fruit that has been off the tree seldom more than a day and you'll generally buy it from the people who grew and picked it, so you can ask for tips about storing the fruit or quiz them on favorite recipes.

What I love best about farmers markets, though, is the fact that the variety of fruits (and other products) you find is often far more diverse and interesting than what you see in most grocery stores. Take Ron and Roslyn Lawrence, for example, owners of R & R Farms in Wenatchee, Washington. They mostly grow luscious apricots, which they pick themselves and bring to the University District and Columbia City farmers markets in Seattle. But on their property are a couple of heritage greengage plum trees that Ron figures were planted back in the 1920s. He thought the trees were dead when they purchased the property in 1980 and had plowed over them, only to find the strong, determined trees coming back to life the following year.

Today, those trees produce 125 pounds or so of fruit each summer. When picked ripe (the only way he'll pick them), the plums offer an explosion of flavor and are highly prized by his market customers. But even from the tree to the farmers market table, Ron says the plums are just so delicate that he loses about 20 percent of the fruit to cracking and bruising. In regular retail channels, these plums would be hopeless and few purveyors would want to risk the loss from damaged fruit. Newer nursery stock of greengage plums produces firmer fruit, but it in no way duplicates the flavor and sweetness of those older trees. You've got to go to a farmers market for those special plums, and I do.

Seattle's fantastic Pike Place Market was founded in 1907 and operates year-round, though the peak experience is May through October when local farmers pile their low-stall tables high with seasonal fruits and vegetables. Those are the same months locals can visit once-weekly neighborhood markets, in the University District, Columbia City, West Seattle, and Lake Forest Park. In Portland, too, there are a few weekly farmers markets in different parts of the city. Vancouver's anchor is the Granville Island Public Market, with seasonal markets in East Vancouver, North Vancouver, and the city's West End.

Sage-Baked Pork Chops with Savory Nectarine-Sage Preserves

Sage is an aromatic herb with plenty of flavor and character, a particularly good pairing with pork. Here, thick chops are baked with onions and minced sage, and served with simple fresh nectarine and sage preserves. The herbal-fruity complement goes perfectly with the rich pork. The preserves are also delicious with roasted leg of lamb, lamb chops, or a sage-rubbed pork tenderloin.

To make easy work of measuring freshly ground pepper, grind the pepper onto a small sheet of waxed paper, then fold the paper and slide the ground pepper down this "chute" into a measuring spoon.

4 thick-cut pork chops
   (about 2½ pounds total)
1 tablespoon minced sage
Salt and freshly ground black pepper

2 tablespoons olive oil
1 cup thinly sliced onion
½ cup dry white wine

Savory Nectarine-Sage Preserves

¼ cup moderately packed
   sage leaves
½ cup boiling water
1 pound nectarines

2 tablespoons sugar
½ teaspoon freshly ground
   black pepper

For the savory nectarine-sage preserves, put the sage leaves in a small heatproof dish, pour the boiling water over, and set aside for 30 minutes.

Peel, pit, and coarsely chop the nectarines and put them in a large, heavy saucepan. Use a potato masher or large slotted spoon to partly crush the fruit. Pour the sage-infused water over the fruit (reserving the sage leaves) and stir in the sugar and pepper with 5 or 6 of the sage leaves. Set the pan over medium-high heat and bring to a boil, stirring constantly. Reduce the heat to medium and cook until the mixture thickens (it will start to sputter), stirring occasionally, 15 to 20 minutes.

Transfer the preserves to a heatproof bowl and set aside while cooking the pork chops.

You can make the preserves up to a week in advance and store in a sealed jar in the refrigerator; bring to room temperature before serving.

Preheat the oven to 375°F.

Sprinkle the pork chops with the minced sage and season with salt and pepper, rubbing the seasonings well into the surface of the chops. Heat the oil in an ovenproof skillet over medium-high heat. When the oil is just beginning to smoke, add the pork chops and cook until well browned, about 2 minutes. Turn the chops over and brown the other side for 2 minutes, then scatter the sliced onion and reserved sage leaves over. Drizzle the wine over everything and transfer the skillet, uncovered, to the oven. Bake until there is just the slightest hint of pink left at the center of the chops, 12 to 15 minutes (if not using thick chops, 10 to 12 minutes may suffice).

Transfer the chops to 4 individual warmed plates. Bring the pan juices to a boil over high heat and reduce to thicken slightly, just a minute or so. Spoon the onion and pan juices over the chops, spoon the nectarine-sage preserves alongside, and serve right away.

Makes 4 servings

Pan-Fried Pepper Steak with Syrah-Cherry Sauce

Pepper steak can sometimes be overwhelming, with such a heavy coating of pepper that you can taste little else. I much prefer a judicious scattering of pepper, though it is best to use hand-crushed pepper that will be in coarser, more dominant pieces than even the most "coarse" setting on pepper grinders. Potatoes, of course, are the ideal accompaniment, perhaps a luxurious au gratin or simple mashed potatoes with a bit of blue cheese whisked in at the end. Rib-eye or T-bone steaks are dandy alternatives to the New York strip called for here.

Cast-iron is a terrific conductor of heat and is the ideal choice for pan-frying steak. Preheat the dense skillet for a few minutes longer than you would other skillets so that it will be at an optimal and consistent heat before you add the steaks. Be prepared for some smoke to rise from the pan, and have the exhaust fan on "high."

2 teaspoons black peppercorns
2 New York strip steaks, about
    ¾ inch thick (1½ pounds total)
Salt
2 tablespoons unsalted butter

2 ounces Bing or other dark
    sweet cherries
1 shallot, minced
½ cup syrah or other dry red wine

Put the peppercorns on a sturdy work surface in a single layer. Set the bottom of a heavy pan over some of the peppercorns and press down firmly, pushing the pan slightly away from you to finely crush the peppercorns. Continue with the remaining peppercorns. Press both sides of the steaks gently into the crushed pepper to lightly but evenly coat them, patting the steaks to help the pepper adhere. Season both sides of the steaks with salt and set aside on a plate.

Heat the butter in a heavy skillet over medium-high heat. When the butter is melted, gently swirl the pan to evenly coat the bottom, then add the steaks. Pan-fry the steaks until they are cooked to taste, about 5 minutes per side for medium-rare to medium. Set the steaks aside on a plate, covered with foil to help keep them warm.

Pit and coarsely chop the cherries. Add the shallot to the skillet and cook over medium heat until tender and aromatic, about 1 minute. Add the wine, stirring to loosen any tasty bits cooked to the bottom of the skillet, then stir in the cherries. Simmer over medium-high heat for a few minutes until the sauce is slightly reduced. Taste for seasoning, adding salt or pepper if needed.

Transfer the steaks to 2 warmed dinner plates, spoon the Syrah-Cherry Sauce over, and serve right away.

Makes 2 servings

Northwest Reds

White wine grapes, particularly riesling and chardonnay, have dominated much of the history of Washington wines. But in recent years, the red wine grapes have steadily been gaining ground against the whites, and in 2000 surpassed white grapes in total production for the first time. Merlot and cabernet sauvignon are by far the top red grapes, but syrah— a relative newcomer to the state—comes in at No. 3 and is steadily growing in appreciation with the state's wine makers. The arid eastern half of the state, with its extremes of cold winters and hot dry summers, is proving itself an ideal territory for growing fully developed, lush grapes that produce equally lush and complex red wines.

Pinot noir has long been the dominant red grape in Oregon, where much of the growing region is in the milder western section of the state, typically more conducive to white grapes (such as pinot gris and chardonnay). Recent statistics from the Oregon Department of Agriculture show that pinot noir accounts for nearly half of the state's total wine grape acreage. Add in merlot, cabernet sauvignon, and other red varietals and Oregon, too, has a majority of red wine production.

Up in the Okanagan Valley, where the vast majority of British Columbia's wine grapes are grown, chardonnay still leads the pack based on 2000 statistics, but red grapes are also on the rise, with merlot, pinot noir, and cabernet franc among the top production in that category. In this relatively young wine-making region, growers are discovering that in the southern reaches of the valley, near the Washington border, the growing conditions are ideal for the lush ripening needed for red wine grapes.

Plum and Shrimp Stir-Fry with Bok Choy and Szechwan Pepper

Once the wok's heated and you toss in the first ingredients, cooking goes very quickly for this recipe. Be sure to have all the elements prepared—the shrimp peeled, plums pitted, and so on—so you won't have to bring everything to a halt in the midst of cooking. Choose light-skinned plums, such as greengage or shiro; darker purple-skinned plums will bleed into the cooking liquids and leave a murky dark finish, though the dish will still be tasty.

Szechwan pepper is the dried berry from the Chinese prickly ash bush, not related to the common black peppercorns we use daily. Szechwan pepper has a distinctive flavor and aroma, not simply a heat profile; if you're unable to find it, you could use ¼ to ½ teaspoon of red pepper flakes to add a touch of heat or simply omit the pepper altogether.

3 tablespoons vegetable oil
¼ cup thinly sliced green onion
1 tablespoon thinly sliced garlic
1 head bok choy, rinsed, dried,
    trimmed, and cut into ½-inch slices
1½ pounds medium shrimp,
    peeled and deveined

1 pound ripe but firm plums,
    pitted and cut into 1-inch wedges
½ to 1 teaspoon Szechwan pepper,
    lightly crushed
Soy sauce
3 cups steamed jasmine rice

Heat 2 tablespoons of the oil in a wok or a large, heavy skillet over medium-high heat. When the oil is just beginning to smoke, add the green onion and garlic and stir-fry until very fragrant, just a few seconds. Add the bok choy and stir-fry until it is just barely tender but still firm, 2 to 3 minutes. Transfer the bok choy to a medium bowl and set aside.

Add the remaining tablespoon of oil to the wok and heat it until nearly smoking. Add the shrimp and toss for a few seconds, then add the plums and stir-fry until the shrimp are just evenly pink, 1 to 2 minutes longer. Return the bok choy to the wok with the Szechwan pepper and a drizzle of soy sauce to taste. Toss to evenly mix the ingredients, about 1 minute. The shrimp should be just barely opaque through and the plums warmed but not falling apart.

Spoon the steamed rice onto 4 individual plates and top with the plum and shrimp stir-fry. Serve right away.

Makes 4 servings

Desserts

Northwest Plum Clafoutis

Typically clafoutis is served at room temperature, not warm, so it can be made just before dinner, or earlier, and it'll be ready to serve come dessert time. Clafoutis is a rustic, simple family-style recipe from France, most commonly made with sweet cherries (which of course you may do, too, particularly sweet Bings). Off-season, the clafoutis could be made with frozen sweet cherries, or other fresh seasonal fruits such as fat blueberries or sliced pears. Though traditionally this dessert is served as is, a finish of crème fraîche or scoop of vanilla ice cream would be a tasty embellishment.

This recipe is based on one I was given by Anne-Marie Choplain, a friend from Dijon, who is responsible for some of my most profound food memories from the time that I lived in France. And, as Burgundy is my adoptive home, so is the Northwest of the United States hers, so the recipe represents a commingling of passions and flavors that makes such international exchanges so delightful.

½ cup plus 1 tablespoon sugar
½ cup all-purpose flour
Pinch salt
1¼ cups milk
3 eggs, lightly beaten

1 teaspoon vanilla extract
1½ pounds plums
1 tablespoon unsalted butter,
    cut into small pieces

Preheat the oven to 425°F. Generously butter a 12-inch oval gratin dish or similar baking dish.

Combine ½ cup of the sugar with the flour and salt in a medium bowl and use a whisk to blend, then whisk in the milk, eggs, and vanilla to make a smooth batter. Pit the plums, cut them into eighths and scatter them evenly over the bottom of the baking dish. Pour the batter over the plums.

Put the clafoutis in the oven and immediately reduce the temperature to 375°F. Bake until the batter is set and lightly browned, about 30 minutes. Take the clafoutis from the oven and sprinkle the remaining tablespoon of sugar over, dotting the top with the butter. Return the pan to the oven and bake until the sugar on top lightly caramelizes, about 10 minutes longer.

Let the clafoutis cool to room temperature. Scoop the clafoutis out onto individual plates and serve.

Makes 6 to 8 servings

Cherry Sorbet Coupe

Think of this dessert as a grown-up ice cream float. Scoops of fresh cherry sorbet are topped with bubbly sparkling wine—such as a Northwest blanc de noir perhaps— a refreshing finish to a summertime meal. The recipe could also be made for a distinctive apéritif before dinner, in which case you should use less of the sorbet to accent the wine, using a large melon baller to form smaller scoops. You could also skip the wine and serve the cherry sorbet alone for dessert, with shortbread or other simple cookies.

1 bottle (750 ml) sparkling wine   Small mint sprigs, for garnish

Cherry Sorbet

½ cup sugar   1 pound Bing or other dark
½ cup water   sweet cherries
                         ¼ cup freshly squeezed lemon juice

For the cherry sorbet, combine the sugar and water in a small saucepan and warm over medium heat, stirring occasionally, until the sugar is dissolved, about 5 minutes. Bring the sugar syrup just to a boil, then take the pan from the heat and set aside to thoroughly cool.

When the syrup is cooled, pit the cherries and purée them in a food processor or blender, then pass through a fine sieve to remove bits of skin, pressing on the solids with the back of a rubber spatula to remove as much juice as possible. Stir in the cooled sugar syrup and lemon juice and refrigerate until fully chilled. Pour the mixture into an ice cream maker and freeze according to the manufacturer's instructions. Transfer the sorbet to a freezer container and freeze until set, at least 2 hours.

Scoop the sorbet, preferably using a small scoop, into champagne flutes or wine glasses. Slowly pour the sparkling wine over, garnish each glass with a sprig of mint, and serve right away.

Makes 8 servings

Deep-Dish Peach Pie

My favorite deep-dish pie pan is the durable unglazed stoneware type, which draws away excess moisture to help avoid sogginess. If you don't have a deep-dish pie pan, you may use a regular pie pan, reducing the amount of peaches to 3 pounds. You may have a bit more crust than needed; roll out excess trimmings, sprinkle with cinnamon and sugar, and bake in a separate pie pan until firm and lightly browned—this extra treat for the baker is one of my fondest memories of cooking with my mom when I was a kid.

The technique described for the lattice topping provides a woven effect, with the strips lying over and under each other. For a quicker, easier option, you may arrange all the horizontal strips as noted and simply lay the vertical strips over the others, without weaving.

4 pounds peaches
½ cup freshly squeezed orange juice
1 teaspoon vanilla extract
¼ cup cornstarch
¼ cup packed light brown sugar
¼ cup sugar

1 teaspoon ground cinnamon
½ teaspoon freshly ground
    or grated nutmeg
1 egg
1 tablespoon water

Pie Crust

3 cups all-purpose flour
¼ cup granulated sugar
2 teaspoons finely grated
    orange zest (optional)
½ teaspoon salt

1 cup unsalted butter,
    cut into pieces and chilled
1 egg yolk
2 tablespoons freshly squeezed
    lemon juice
5 to 6 tablespoons ice water

For the pie crust, combine the flour, sugar, orange zest (if using), and salt in a food processor and pulse once to mix. Add the chilled butter pieces and pulse until the butter is finely chopped and the flour mixture has a coarse sandy texture. Add the egg yolk and lemon juice, pulse once, and then add the water one tablespoon at a time, pulsing once or twice after each addition. It's important not to overmix the dough or it will be tough rather than flaky. The dough will not form a ball in the machine, but has the proper amount of liquid if when you squeeze some of the dough between your fingers, it feels neither dusty dry nor sticky. Turn the dough out onto a work surface and form it into a ball. Cut the dough into 2 pieces, one larger than the other (about ⅔ to ⅓), form into discs about 1 inch thick, and wrap in plastic. Refrigerate the dough for at least 30 minutes before rolling it out.

Preheat the oven to 375°F.

Bring a large pan of water to a boil. When the water boils, add a few peaches to the water and boil until the skin begins to split, about 30 seconds. Scoop out the peaches with a slotted spoon and let cool while blanching the remaining peaches.

Put the orange juice and vanilla in a large bowl. Working with one peach at a time, peel away the skin, pit the peach, and cut it into 1-inch slices. Add the slices to the bowl, tossing gently to coat with the orange juice, which will help keep the peaches from discoloring. Continue with the remaining peaches, tossing each gently with the others in the bowl. When all the peaches have been sliced, sprinkle the cornstarch, brown sugar, granulated sugar, cinnamon, and nutmeg over the peaches and quickly toss to coat them evenly. Set aside while preparing the crust.

Remove the larger dough portion from the refrigerator and roll it out on a lightly floured board to a circle about 15 inches across (let the dough sit for a few minutes to soften just a bit if it's too firm to roll out). Line a 10-inch deep-dish pie pan with the dough so that the overhang is more or less even all around and press the dough down gently into the corners. Carefully toss the peach mixture one last time, and then spoon it into the crust, mounding it slightly in the center.

Roll out the remaining dough portion to a circle about 12 inches across. Using a fluted pastry cutter, a pizza cutter, or a sharp knife and a clean straight-edge as a guide, cut the dough into strips about ¾ inch wide. Lay some of the strips across the peach filling horizontally, leaving about a 1 inch gap between each. Fold every-other strip back on top of itself just to the midpoint of the filling. Lay another long strip perpendicularly across the remaining strips and up against those folded strips. Unfold the folded strips over that new strip, and fold back the alternate strips, folding them back to the point where the perpendicular strip is covering them. Again, lay a new strip across the remaining strips. Repeat this process, folding back the alternating halves of strips until you reach the outer edge of the crust. Do the same from the center out to the other edge of the crust.

Combine the egg and water in a small bowl and beat with a fork to blend, making an egg wash for the pie crust. Using kitchen shears or a small knife, trim the lattice strip ends to lie about ½ inch over the bottom crust edge. Brush the crust edge and the lattice topping lightly with the egg wash. Trim the bottom crust overhang to about 1 inch and fold it up over the lattice ends to fully enclose them. Using the tines of a fork or your fingers, crimp the edges of the crust to firmly seal and make a decorative finish. Brush the crust rim again with egg wash.

Bake the pie until the crust is well browned and the filling is bubbling up through the lattice, about 1 hour. In case the filling bubbles over the edge of the pan, you might want to place a baking sheet on the rack below the pie to catch drips. Lay a piece of foil loosely over the pie if the crust gets well browned before the pie is fully cooked. Let the pie cool on a wire rack for at least 30 minutes before cutting into wedges to serve.

Makes 8 to 12 servings

The base of these delicious bar cookies is much like shortbread, with something of a biscuity topping and an amber layer of apricot purée sandwiched between. Dried apricots are a great off-season alternative: use ¾ pound dried fruit plumped in hot water for an hour or two before draining and puréeing. I've also prepared this recipe with half dried apricots and half dried figs, a tasty alternative.

3 cups all-purpose flour	¾ cup sugar
½ teaspoon salt	1 teaspoon baking powder
1 cup unsalted butter, at room temperature	1 egg
	¼ cup milk

Apricot Filling

1½ pounds apricots	2 tablespoons freshly squeezed
1 cup sugar	lemon juice

Preheat the oven to 300°F.

For the apricot filling, halve and pit the apricots and set them cut-side up on a baking sheet. Bake them for 30 minutes to draw off some of the excess moisture. Turn the apricots cut-side down onto a double layer of paper towels until cool. Purée the apricots in a food processor with the sugar and lemon juice until smooth, scraping down the sides as needed. Transfer the purée to a bowl and set aside.

Increase the oven temperature to 350°F. Butter and flour a 9-by-13-inch baking dish.

Sift together the flour and salt into a bowl. Cream together the butter and sugar with an electric mixer at medium speed until well blended and fluffy. Working at low speed, gradually add the flour mixture until evenly blended. Spoon 4 cups of the mixture into the prepared baking dish and set aside. Sift the baking powder over the remaining dough in the bowl and use a fork to evenly mix it into the dough. Add the egg and milk, and stir with the fork to blend the ingredients. (Overmixing will toughen the dough, so don't use the mixer at this point.) This mixture will be used as a topping for the bars.

Spread the dough in the baking dish to an even layer, and then press down firmly to make a solid base. Pour the apricot purée over the base and spread out to an even layer. Use a small spoon to randomly scatter the dough topping over the surface of the apricot purée.

Bake the apricot bars until the base is baked through and the topping is puffed and lightly browned, about 40 minutes. Let cool completely before cutting the pastry into squares.

Makes 15 to 18 bars

Grilled Peach Melba with Peach Ice Cream

Melding together a couple of peachy favorites—Melba and ice cream—this recipe is a peach nirvana to enjoy when the fruit is at its peak of flavor and sweetness. Grilling peaches may sound a bit unusual, but the few minutes on the grill only gently warms the fruit and lightly caramelizes the cut surface, further emphasizing the luscious flavor. Plan this dessert for a meal that has the grill in use already, though you may also skip the grilling and simply serve the halved fresh peaches as is.

For a more traditional Melba, omit the peach ice cream and either make classic vanilla (omitting the peach and lemon juice mixture) or use top-quality store-bought ice cream.

3 large ripe but firm peaches   1 teaspoon vegetable oil

Peach Ice Cream

1 vanilla bean, split lengthwise,
    or 1 teaspoon vanilla extract
2½ cups half-and-half
6 egg yolks

¾ cup sugar
2 large peaches
Juice of 1 small lemon
1 cup whipping cream, well chilled

Raspberry Sauce

1 pint fresh raspberries,
    or frozen raspberries, thawed
¼ cup powdered sugar or more to taste

1 tablespoon kirsch (cherry brandy,
    optional)

For the peach ice cream, combine the vanilla bean with the half-and-half in a medium saucepan and bring it just to a boil over medium-high heat. Take the pan from the heat and set aside, covered, for 30 minutes. Lift the vanilla bean from the milk and set it on the work surface. Run the back of a small knife down the length of the inside of the bean to remove the tiny seeds and add them to the milk. If using vanilla extract instead, simply bring the milk to a boil and proceed; the vanilla extract will be added later.

In a medium bowl, combine the egg yolks with the sugar and whisk until well blended and beginning to turn pale yellow. Slowly whisk the warm milk into the egg mixture, then pour this back into the saucepan with the vanilla extract, if using. Cook the custard over medium heat, stirring constantly with a wooden spoon, until the mixture has thickened enough to coat the back of the spoon, 7 to 10 minutes. Take the custard from the heat and let cool; then refrigerate until well chilled.

When the custard is chilled, peel and pit the peaches and coarsely chop them. Put the peaches in a food processor with the lemon juice and pulse to finely chop them. I like to keep some peachy texture, so try to avoid thoroughly puréeing the peaches. Stir the peaches into the custard base. Whip the cream until lightly thickened (you don't need to whip the cream enough to form peaks) and fold it into the ice cream base until thoroughly blended. Freeze in an ice-cream maker according to manufacturer's instructions. Transfer the ice cream to a freezer container and freeze until set, at least 2 hours.

For the raspberry sauce, combine the berries, powdered sugar, and kirsch (if using) in a food processor or blender and purée until smooth. Strain the sauce through a fine sieve to remove the raspberry seeds, then taste for seasoning, adding a bit more powdered sugar if needed. Refrigerate until ready to serve.

Preheat an outdoor grill. Pit the peaches and rub each cut half lightly with oil. When the grill is heated, lightly brush the grill grate with oil and set the peaches on the hot grill, cut-side down. Grill just until the peach is lightly browned and marked by the grill, 2 to 3 minutes.

Scoop some of the Peach Ice Cream into large bowls and set a grilled peach half alongside. Drizzle the Raspberry Sauce over all and serve right away.

Makes 6 servings

Nectarine and Hazelnut Meringues

Crisp meringues make a nutty-delicious edible container for sweet nectarines. The amount of Frangelico (a hazelnut liqueur) needed for this recipe is just the quantity you find in those minibottles, if you don't want to commit to purchasing a larger bottle. The liqueur adds a touch of nutty sweetness to slices of juicy nectarines, used to fill equally nutty-sweet hazelnut meringues.

¾ cup (about 4 ounces) hazelnuts
3 egg whites
¾ cup sugar
3 large nectarines

¼ cup Frangelico (hazelnut liqueur)
   or hazelnut syrup
¾ cup whipping cream

Preheat the oven to 350°F.

Scatter the hazelnuts in a baking pan and toast until lightly browned and aromatic, about 8 to 10 minutes, gently shaking the pan once or twice to help the nuts toast evenly. Transfer the nuts to a slightly dampened dish towel, fold the towel completely over the nuts and vigorously rub them to remove as much of the papery skins as possible. Set aside to cool, then finely chop the hazelnuts either by hand or in a food processor. (If using the food processor, add 1 tablespoon of the sugar and pulse until the nuts are mostly finely chopped; avoid overprocessing or the nuts will form a paste, which won't blend well with the meringue.)

Reduce the oven temperature to 225°F. Cut a piece of parchment paper to line a baking sheet. Draw 6 circles 4 inches in diameter on the paper, with at least 1 inch between them.

Whip the egg whites with an electric mixer at high speed until they are quite frothy and begin to hold soft peaks. With the mixer running at medium speed, slowly add the sugar and continue beating until the meringue is glossy and holds stiff peaks when the beater is lifted. Sprinkle half of the finely chopped hazelnuts over and gently fold them into the meringue until evenly blended, then repeat with the rest of the nuts.

Secure the parchment paper to the baking sheet with a tiny bit of meringue under each corner. Spoon the meringue into the circles drawn on the paper and use the back of the spoon to form cups with sides about an inch high and a solid base that's not too thin. Don't be too worried about making perfect circles with perfect edges; you just want the meringues to have a bit of an indentation to hold the fruit. Bake the meringues until they are firm and lightly browned, about 2 hours.

While the meringues are baking, pit and slice the nectarines. Put the slices in a large bowl and drizzle with 3 tablespoons of the Frangelico. Toss gently and refrigerate until ready to serve, stirring occasionally.

Take the baked meringues from the oven and let cool for a few minutes on the baking sheet, then carefully lift the meringues from the paper to fully cool on a cake rack.

Shortly before serving, whip the cream until soft peaks form, then add the remaining tablespoon of Frangelico and continue whipping until well blended.

To serve, set each meringue on an individual plate. Spoon the sliced nectarines into the meringues, drizzling with the soaking liquids. Top with a generous dollop of whipped cream and serve right away.

Makes 6 servings

Oregon Hazelnuts: The state of Oregon is by far the country's largest producer of hazelnuts, growing more than 99 percent of the national crop of this delicious little nut. Also known as the filbert, the hazelnut became the state's official nut in 1989.

The first hazelnut tree in Oregon is said to have been planted by an Englishman, a retiree from the Hudson's Bay Company, in 1858 in the Umpqua Valley of the southern part of the state. Frenchman David Gernot is credited with planting the first grove of fifty hazelnut trees a couple of decades later, farther north in the Willamette Valley. Today, there are well over three million hazelnut trees in Oregon, most of them still in the state's prolific Willamette Valley. The Nut Growers Society uses a gavel that was made from the region's first hazelnut tree, a testament to the importance the nut has played in the region over so many years.

These nuts are wonderfully versatile, as well suited to a savory salad with blue cheese as to a dessert with fruit or ice cream. In addition to whole nuts, you'll find Oregon hazelnuts making their way into hazelnut butter, dry-roasted nuts, chocolate-covered hazelnuts, and hazelnut oil, among many other foods.

Plum Galettes

This divine but simple recipe is easy and adaptable: you may use quartered apricots or sliced nectarines or peaches in place of the plums. The layer of frangipane, a sweetened almond paste, adds a nutty richness to the simple flat tartlets. Puff pastry should be thawed slowly in the refrigerator, preferably overnight, so plan ahead with your shopping. This fruit dessert is delightful as is, but you could top each serving with a small scoop of vanilla ice cream, if you like.

¼ cup whole blanched almonds
   (about 1½ ounces)
3 tablespoons sugar
2 tablespoons all-purpose flour
2 tablespoons unsalted butter,
   at room temperature

1 egg
¼ teaspoon almond extract (optional)
1 pound frozen puff pastry, thawed
¾ to 1 pound ripe but firm plums

Preheat the oven to 400°F. Line 2 baking sheets with parchment paper.

Put the almonds in a food processor with the sugar and flour and process until the almonds are very finely ground. Add the butter, egg, and almond extract, if using, and pulse a few times to evenly blend, scraping down the sides as needed. Transfer the frangipane to a bowl and set aside.

Unfold one portion of the puff pastry on a lightly floured work surface and roll gently just to even out the dough (you don't need to make it much thinner than it is already). Using a pan lid as a guide, cut two 6-inch circles from the pastry and transfer them to a parchment-lined baking sheet. Repeat with the other half of the dough.

Spread the frangipane evenly over the circles, leaving the outer ½ inch clear. Pit and quarter the plums. Arrange the plum pieces skin-side down on the frangipane, in a round pattern.

Bake the galettes until the plums are tender and the pastry is well puffed and browned, 15 to 20 minutes. Transfer each galette to an individual plate and serve right away, or let cool on a wire rack and serve at room temperature.

Makes 4 servings

Cherry Cheesecake Tart with Gingersnap Crust

When pitted and chopped dark sweet cherries are added to this cheesecake batter, they give the snow-white mixture a rosy pink blush. Gingersnaps make a tasty change from the traditional graham-cracker crust, though because the cookies are so hard you'll need to work a bit more to make the crumbs. Smash the gingersnaps first in a heavy plastic bag, then pulse them in a food processor to form the crumbs. You may use graham crackers instead, if you like. Frozen pitted cherries are a great substitute for fresh here.

2½ cups gingersnap crumbs
(about half of a 1 pound box)
½ cup unsalted butter, melted
1 pound cream cheese,
at room temperature
½ cup sugar
2 eggs

½ teaspoon almond extract or
1 teaspoon vanilla extract
¾ pound Bing or other dark
sweet cherries
2 ounces white chocolate,
melted (optional)

Preheat the oven to 350°F.

In a medium bowl, combine the gingersnap crumbs and butter and stir to mix evenly. Put the crumb mixture in a 9- to 10-inch quiche pan or deep pie pan and press the crumbs into the bottom and sides of the pan to make a solid crust. Bake the gingersnap shell until set, about 5 minutes. Set aside to cool; leave the oven set at 350°F.

Whip the cream cheese and sugar with an electric beater at medium speed until well blended. Add the eggs and almond extract and continue beating until fully incorporated to make a smooth batter, scraping down the sides of the bowl as needed. Pit and quarter the cherries, add them to the cream cheese mixture, and beat at low speed for a minute or so, to blend evenly and lightly tint the batter.

Pour the batter into the cooled crust and spread it out evenly. Bake the tart until the cheesecake is set, about 35 minutes (the center may be slightly jiggly, but the outer portions should be firm). Set aside on a wire rack to cool completely, then refrigerate for at least 2 hours before serving. Shortly before serving, drizzle the melted white chocolate, if using, over the top of the tart in a random pattern. Cut the tart into pieces and serve.

Makes 8 to 12 servings

Chilled Nectarine Soup with Late-Harvest Wine

Liquid deliciousness, this recipe combines juicy nectarines with nectarlike late-harvest wine, made from extraripe grapes with concentrated sweetness and flavor. This recipe may also be made with white or yellow peaches, or a combination of both, using one white-fleshed fruit for the final garnish on the otherwise soft yellow-orange soup. Choose a not-too-expensive late-harvest wine to give the soup its distinctive flavor while saving a more prized bottle for sipping alongside. Most of these wines come in 375 ml bottles, the perfect size for this recipe.

2½ pounds nectarines
1½ cups late-harvest riesling
   or gewürztraminer
1 cup dry white wine
½ cup sugar

¼ cup freshly squeezed lemon juice
2 sprigs lemon verbena or
   lemon thyme or ½ teaspoon
   grated lemon zest
½ cup whipping cream

Pit all but one of the nectarines and put the halves in a large saucepan. Set aside ¼ cup of the late-harvest wine for later and add the rest to the pan with the dry white wine, sugar, lemon juice, and lemon verbena. Add about 2 cups of water so that the liquid just covers the nectarines. Bring the liquid just to a boil over high heat, then reduce the heat to medium and gently simmer until the nectarines are tender when poked with the tip of a knife, 15 to 20 minutes.

Take the pan from the heat and set aside to cool. When cool, remove and discard the lemon verbena. Slip off and discard the skin from the nectarine halves and transfer them to a food processor or blender with about ½ cup of the poaching liquid. Process until smooth, then put the purée in a bowl and stir in the remaining poaching liquid. Refrigerate until well chilled, at least 2 hours or up to 24 hours.

Shortly before serving, whip the cream until soft peaks begin to form, then drizzle in the remaining ¼ cup of late-harvest wine and continue whipping until well blended. Pit and finely chop the remaining nectarine. Ladle the soup into shallow soup bowls, scatter the chopped nectarine over and drizzle the whipped cream over in a random pattern. Serve right away.

Makes 6 servings

Rice Pudding with Cherries

Some rice pudding recipes are fully cooked stovetop, but my mom always baked her rice pudding, so that is my preferred method as well. It's okay to use leftover rice, though the rice will lose some of its aroma and flavor after a few days, so for best results plan on making the rice fresh. You may use regular long-grain rice or, for a delicate aroma, choose basmati or jasmine rice.

Frozen sweet cherries are a great option for preparing this dish in the off-season. Chop them up while they're still frozen; they'll be firm and easier to handle. You could use dried sweet cherries also, about ¾ cup, plumped first in hot water, then well drained.

2 cups milk
Pinch salt
¾ cup long-grain rice
2 eggs
½ cup sugar
1½ cups half-and-half or heavy cream,
    plus extra for serving (optional)

1 teaspoon vanilla extract
½ teaspoon ground cinnamon
Pinch freshly grated or ground nutmeg
¾ pound Bing or other dark
    sweet cherries

Preheat the oven to 350°F. Generously butter a 6-cup baking dish.

Put the milk in a medium saucepan with the salt and bring just to a boil over medium-high heat. Reduce the heat to medium-low and stir in the rice. Cover the pan and cook until the rice has absorbed most of the liquid, about 20 minutes. Remove the lid and stir the rice gently, then set aside for about 15 minutes to cool slightly, stirring occasionally.

In a medium bowl, whisk the eggs with the sugar until well blended, then whisk in the half-and-half, vanilla, cinnamon, and nutmeg. Pit and coarsely chop the cherries, then add them to the rice with the egg mixture. Stir with a wooden spoon until evenly mixed.

Spoon the rice pudding into the prepared baking dish and bake until the pudding is set and the top is browned, about 1 hour. Let cool slightly before spooning into bowls to serve. Pass extra half-and-half or cream, if desired, for pouring over the warm pudding.

Makes 6 to 8 servings

Beverages

Rosé Sangria

I've always felt that rosé wines are the essence of summer (and I know I'm not the only one). They're light, bright, fruity, and not at all fussy—the perfect summer sipper to enjoy on the patio or at the cabin, with simple grilled food or other casual fare.

The blush of Rainier cherries is especially suited to this sangria. You could use Bings or other dark sweet cherries instead, but they'll bleed their darker juice and alter the wine's soft pink color. This drink would be a great use for white-fleshed peach or nectarine, the pale flesh playing off the other colors in the sangria.

¼ cup water	1 nectarine or peach
3 tablespoons sugar	½ lime, thinly sliced
2 bottles (750 ml each) dry rosé wine	¼ cup brandy or kirsch
½ pound Rainier cherries	1 cup club soda

In a small saucepan, combine the water and sugar and warm over medium heat, stirring occasionally, until the sugar has dissolved, 3 to 5 minutes. Increase the heat to high and bring just to a boil, then set the sugar syrup aside to cool.

Pour the rosé into a large pitcher, preferably glass. Pit and halve the cherries and add them to the wine. Pit and thinly slice the nectarine and add it to the pitcher with the lime slices. Stir in the brandy and sugar syrup, then chill the sangria until ready to serve, ideally a few hours to allow the fruit flavors to blend with the wine.

Just before serving, stir in the club soda, and then pour the chilled sangria into large wine glasses, spooning some of the fruit into each serving.

Makes 10 to 12 servings

The Ultimate Peach Milkshake

This delicious milkshake tastes something like a Creamsicle, but with a fresh peach twist. I like the blend of peach nectar and fresh peach because of the layering of flavors. Though simply a satisfying snack on a hot summer afternoon, the drink could also be dressed up for a fun, casual dessert with friends, perhaps spiked with brandy or dark rum, and served with cookies. Look for peach nectar on the grocery shelves with other canned and bottled juices.

1 peach	½ cup peach nectar, more if needed
1½ cups top-quality vanilla ice cream	½ cup freshly squeezed orange juice

Pit and slice the peach, setting aside 2 thin slices for garnish. Put the remaining peach slices in a blender with the ice cream, peach nectar, and orange juice and blend until very smooth. If the shake is quite thick, add a few tablespoons more peach nectar or orange juice.

Pour the peach shake into two tall glasses, garnish each with a peach slice, and serve right away.

Makes 2 servings

Manhattan with Spiked Cherries

I prefer my Manhattans "perfect," which doesn't refer to their quality but to the vermouth used. A classic Manhattan uses only sweet vermouth, a dry Manhattan only dry vermouth; the "perfect" Manhattan uses equal parts of each. Dried sweet cherries work well in this recipe, since they're available year-round and their concentrated flavor is well suited to this strong, flavorful drink. But fresh cherries are a luscious option when they're in season.

If you're a big Manhattan fan, or plan to have a party, you'll be glad to have a good supply of presoaked cherries ready to go (this recipe makes enough for 8 to 12 cocktails). They'll keep for a month or more in the refrigerator; add a bit more bourbon as needed so the cherries remain fully covered. If you use fresh cherries, simply soak enough pitted cherries so that you'll have one for each cocktail you plan to make that evening; an hour or two of soaking is plenty for fresh cherries.

2 fluid ounces (¼ cup) bourbon
½ fluid ounce (1 tablespoon) sweet
   vermouth

½ fluid ounce (1 tablespoon)
   dry vermouth
Dash angostura bitters

Spiked Cherries

8 to 12 fresh sweet cherries
   or ¼ cup dried cherries

½ cup bourbon

If using dried cherries, prepare the spiked cherries at least a day ahead: in a small, clean jar combine the cherries and bourbon. Cover tightly with the lid, shake gently to mix, and refrigerate until ready to serve. For fresh cherries, pit the cherries an hour or two before serving and put them in a small bowl with the bourbon and let sit until ready to use.

Fill a cocktail shaker with ice and pour the bourbon, sweet and dry vermouth, and bitters over the ice. Add a teaspoon or so of the spiked cherry liquid. Top the shaker with the lid and vigorously shake the ingredients to blend. Strain the mixture into a chilled martini glass, add one spiked fresh cherry or a few spiked dried cherries to the glass (they'll be a treat waiting at the bottom when the cocktail is finished), and serve right away.

Makes 1 serving

The Maraschino Cherry

The maraschino cherry has its origins on the Dalmatian Coast (in what is now known as Croatia) and in northern Italy, going back more than a few centuries. Maraschino cherries get their name from a cherry that is native in that region, called *marasca*, which had long been preserved in a locally produced cherry liqueur, which also goes by the name "maraschino." But the modern-day maraschino cherry that tops endless ice cream sundaes and garnishes many a cocktail can be credited to an innovative professor at Oregon Agricultural College (now Oregon State University).

As trade routes grew to crisscross the globe, those original maraschino cherries eventually made their way to the United States and became all the rage in restaurants and homes of the well-to-do in the late nineteenth century. Fast-forward to the 1920s, when Oregon State University professor E. H. Wiegand developed a new technique for making maraschino cherries, using the local Royal Ann cherry.

It's said that part of what prompted this development was an overabundance of cherries one year, necessity once again proving to be the mother of invention. There is a lot of science in the making of a maraschino cherry, but suffice it to say that Wiegand modernized the procedure to boost the firm, plump character of the cherries and help produce more reliable results, part of which was due to his addition of calcium to the process. Techniques based on that research are still in use today, and OSU memorialized the professor's contribution with the naming of Wiegand Hall, one of the Food Sciences & Technology buildings on the Corvallis campus.

But the maraschino cherry isn't just a historic footnote at OSU. Research continues at the school, one recent area of attention on the coloration of the cherries. Experts are working to develop a natural colorant that will still produce the vivid red color consumers expect in a maraschino but with the benefits—such as antioxidant—of natural pigments (one potential source being the radish).

Peach Daiquiris

This all-about-the-peaches cocktail is a great way to enjoy the fruit at its peak of ripeness. I first tasted this daiquiri (rumless) at the opening day of Peach-o-Rama at Seattle's Queen Anne Thriftway. The recipe is credited to Tom Pence, owner of Pence Orchards in Wapato, Washington, source of some of the premium peaches that are featured during this month-long peach extravaganza (see page 22 for more on Pence Orchards).

I've adapted the recipe slightly, adding the traditional rum and using fresh lime juice in place of bottled. Peeling peaches makes for a smoother daiquiri, though you may skip that step and leave the skins on; just be sure to purée the peaches well so that the skin is finely minced, which adds a nice flecked effect to the finished drink.

2 large peaches	Ice cubes
½ cup freshly squeezed lime juice	1 cup white rum (optional)
¼ cup sugar, more to taste	Lime slices, for garnish

Pit and coarsely chop the peaches. Combine the peaches, lime juice, and sugar in a blender and blend until very smooth. Taste for sweetness, adding a bit more sugar if needed to suit your taste. Add a handful of ice cubes and continue blending until the ice is fully incorporated. Finally, add the rum, if using, and blend a few seconds longer.

Pour the mixture into tall glasses and serve right away, with a slice of lime on the rim of each glass.

Makes 4 servings

Port and Plum Mulled Wine

In the outdoor-loving Northwest, part of enjoying the great outdoors is the nestling down and warming up when you get back indoors. This mulled wine—embellished with plum brandy and plum quarters—is an ideal beverage for après-ski or any time you need to warm up after a good chill outdoors. Make a fire and settle in, since this mulled wine does pack a punch. Any kind of plum may be used, though sweeter prune-plums are a particularly good choice.

Clear Creek Distillery in Portland, Oregon, distills the best of Northwest fruit in an array of outstanding brandies. Their Blue Plum Brandy is made from Italian blue plums grown in the Yamhill Valley to the southwest of Portland.

1 bottle (750 ml) full-bodied red wine, such as merlot or cabernet-merlot blend

1 cup tawny port

½ cup plum brandy or regular brandy

½ navel orange, thinly sliced

2 strips pared lemon zest

2 cinnamon sticks

4 whole cloves

4 plums

In a large nonreactive saucepan, combine the wine, port, brandy, orange slices, lemon zest, cinnamon sticks, and cloves and stir to mix.

Pit and quarter the plums, add them to the pan, and set the pan over medium heat. Warm just until wisps of steam rise from the pan, about 15 minutes. You don't want the mixture to boil. The mulled wine can be prepared in advance and set aside, then gently rewarmed just before serving. The flavor will further develop as it sits.

Ladle the mulled wine into warmed heatproof glasses or mugs, distributing the plum pieces and orange slices evenly among the servings. Serve right away.

Makes 6 to 8 servings

Apricot Mojito

The mojito, which has taken urban bars by storm, is a vibrant and refreshing Cuban cocktail of lime juice, rum, and mint, with a touch of sugar. This apricot variation is based on a recipe from my friend, chef Kathy Casey, a cocktail maven if ever there was one. She develops cocktails for restaurants and bars around the country from her Food Studios in the Seattle neighborhood of Ballard, where you can also take classes in the art of the cocktail (and the cocktail party!). Peak-season apricots are the best choice for their aromatic, sweet flavor; you may also use a ripe peach or nectarine here, using one quarter of the larger fruit in place of the whole apricot. The fresh lime sweet & sour can be made up to 2 weeks in advance and refrigerated in a well-sealed jar. The recipe makes about 1 cup, enough for 4 mojitos.

1 apricot	1½ teaspoons apricot brandy
3 big sprigs mint	Fresh Lime Sweet & Sour (recipe below)
2 fluid ounces (¼ cup) white rum	Splash soda water

Fresh Lime Sweet & Sour

⅓ cup sugar	½ cup strained freshly
⅓ cup water	squeezed lime juice

For the fresh lime sweet & sour, combine the sugar and water in a small saucepan and warm over medium heat, stirring until the sugar is dissolved, 2 to 3 minutes. Increase the heat to high and bring just to a boil, then take the pan from the heat and let cool completely. When the sugar syrup is cooled, stir in the lime juice.

Peel and pit the apricot, put it in a cocktail shaker, and mash it well with a muddler or wooden spoon. Lightly crush 2 of the mint sprigs between your fingers and add them to the cocktail shaker. Fill the shaker with ice and pour in the rum and apricot brandy, with 2 fluid ounces (¼ cup) of the cooled lime sweet & sour. Vigorously shake for 30 seconds or so. Fill a tall glass with ice and drop in the remaining mint sprig. Strain the mojito over the ice, top with a splash of soda water, and serve.

Makes 1 serving

Northwest Mint: One of the lesser-known top agricultural products of the Northwest is mint. But if you drive through Washington's Yakima Valley with the windows open—as I did one recent summer weekend—you'll catch unmistakable whiffs of minty perfume in the air during harvest. Oregon and Washington are the No. 1 producers of peppermint and spearmint oil in the United States, most of which is used in commercial products such as toothpaste, mouthwash, and chewing gum. A very small part of the harvest is in the form of leaves to be dried for tea, but almost none of this mint makes it to local markets for our culinary uses.

The water-loving plant grows prolifically in the moist Northwest climate, making it a great addition to the herb garden. There is a wide variety of mints to enjoy, from chocolate mint to pineapple mint, so have some fun in the garden, and in the kitchen, experimenting. Consider trying a "Northwest" julep, smashing mint with sugar and ice in a shaker, then topping with 2 ounces of your favorite bourbon before straining over ice with a little sprig of mint for garnish. You could also muddle a few pitted cherries or some chopped peach or apricot with the mint and sugar, adding a touch of fruity aroma to the minty freshness of the cocktail.

Cooking with Stone Fruit

Buying and Storing Stone Fruit

It's tempting to judge a stone fruit by its cover, but considering skin color alone isn't the best indication of ripeness. In the case of peaches and nectarines, for instance, the skin tones vary from variety to variety, so one fruit that is paler than another may not necessarily be less ripe. The same is certainly true of plums, which come in a rainbow of colors from soft green and yellow through an array of red-to-purple varieties to some that seem nearly black.

Where color can be a cue—the background color in the case of fruits that are mottled or have layering of color—is with regard to the color's consistency. A glance at the stem end of the fruit can be telling, too, especially for apricots, nectarines, and peaches. If the skin immediately around the stem area is quite green, the fruit was most surely harvested before it reached maturity on the tree. Though it will eventually soften and may seem to ripen, fruit harvested when immature never really will. These fruits— woolly bland peaches, for instance—are the bane of a fruit-lover's existence, so it pays to understand how stone fruits ripen and how to make good choices when you shop, which I'll discuss below.

In general, the skin of stone fruit should be even and taut, without wrinkles, punctures, or bruises. Ripe peaches, nectarines, apricots, and plums will give gently when pressed, but don't forcefully poke the fruit to check, which may cause bruising. I prefer to instead cradle the fruit in my palm and give it a gentle squeeze with my whole hand to sense the tenderness of the fruit. A good, ripe fruit will also smell enticing, offering up a whiff of its essence even through the skin, especially near the stem end. Aromatic agents (esters) are among the ripeness elements that continue to develop after mature fruit is harvested.

Consider how soon you expect to use the fruit and how you'll be using it. Some recipes, such as Peach Ice Cream (page 70), will be best with fruit that has a maximum of flavor and aroma, no extra points for beauty, so you may choose fruit that is quite ripe and even may have minor blemishes. Other recipes (such as the Beef and Apricot Saté on page 43) call for fruit that is ripe but firm—fruit that is flavorful but sturdy enough to hold up during cooking.

Cherries are picked fully ripe, so choosing cherries is mostly a question of avoiding ones that are damaged or beyond ripe. Pick over cherries to avoid those with split skin or bruises. Take a look at the stem end, where decay can set in first (especially if the stem's been removed), and check that there isn't any bruising or browning.

When you get home, store fresh stone fruit at room temperature, in a produce bag or in a bowl or a basket. Not only will the ambient temperature encourage the continued ripening of the fruit, but the flavor of the fruit will be fuller when it's eaten at room temperature rather than chilled, which dulls flavor.

Once the fruit is fully ripe and ready to eat, do your best to enjoy it soon (within a day or so), or move the fruit to the refrigerator where the lower temperature will retard the ripening effect and prolong the life of the fruit by a few days. Cherries, since they are fully ripe when you buy them, may be stored at room temperature for a day or two, or refrigerated for up to a week.

Stone Fruit Ripeness

When it comes to harvesting fruit, maturity is a more important factor than ripeness. To reach maturity, a fruit needs to fully develop on the tree, taking in nourishment transferred through the branches up to an optimal level of growth that will assure the fruit's capacity for ripeness.

Peaches, nectarines, apricots, and plums are "climacteric" fruits, meaning that they will continue to develop flavor, aroma, and sweetness after they have been harvested. But this will happen only if the fruit is harvested when mature, ensuring that it has enough reserves of starch to fuel its continued ripening postharvest. If not, it will expire before full ripeness is achieved. Fruit that is mature but not yet ripe can get a ripeness boost if you store it in a paper bag with ethylene-producing fruits, such as apples, bananas, or ripe stone fruits for a day or two.

Cherries are a different matter, even more delicate than the other stone fruits. Cherries are "nonclimacteric," so what you pick is what you get. There is no starch to speak of in mature cherries, so they have no means by which to develop further flavor or sweetness once picked. Because they are picked fully ripe, they are even more susceptible to damage in transport than are other stone fruits. Great care must be taken in handling and packing cherries to ensure that the fruit gets to the customer still at its peak.

Some growers opt for picking their fruit tree-ripe, meaning that if you stood in the orchard, plucked the fruit from the tree and sank your teeth into it right away, you'd find it had all the characteristics of a fully ripened fruit. In fact, that's just how the picking time is often chosen, the grower taking a bite and giving the "yea" or "nay" to pickers if happy with the flavor. These fruits are gently hand-picked and collected in shallow foam-bottomed pails, then packed into single layered boxes, since their postharvest stamina is a bit less than that of fruit picked mature rather than ripe.

At the other end of the spectrum are fruits picked "shipping ripe" by growers whose priority is more the durability of the fruit than its flavor quality. These rock-hard fruits are often picked so early that they may be immature and unable to achieve a level of ripeness worth the price paid. Again, look for the telltale green coloring, especially around the stem end, and avoid fruit that doesn't show any of the choice characteristics of ripeness.

Preparing Stone Fruit

Pitting: Most of the peaches, nectarines, apricots, and many plum varieties cultivated today are freestone, meaning that the flesh will easily separate from the pit, which is helpful when preparing fruit for recipes. Clingstone fruits tend to be best for eating fresh out of hand, or are reserved for canning or other commercial production for which pits are removed mechanically.

To pit nectarines, peaches, plums, and apricots, begin by halving the fruit. Starting at the top (stem end), cut into the fruit with a paring knife until you feel the pit under the blade, then draw the knife around the full circumference of the fruit, keeping the blade edge against the pit. When you've cut through the fruit all the way around, hold each half in one hand and gently twist the halves in opposite directions to separate them, then lift out the pit. If you cut the fruit along the slight crease that generally runs down one side of the fruit, you'll halve it so that the pit is lying flat and is much easier to remove.

Fruit that is not very ripe or has a clingy pit will resist being halved. What I tend to do in this case is repeat the cutting step at the midpoint of the halves, quartering the fruit. It can be easier to force off one of these quarters, and then use the tip of the paring knife to help dislodge the other quarters of the fruit. It may be a bit messy, but it'll get the job done.

Pitting cherries is a bit more of a chore, especially when you're preparing a couple of pounds or more for pies or canning. And you really do need the proper tool—a cherry pitter—to do the job. Cherry pitters come in many forms but aren't very expensive, and it is one gadget that will definitely earn its keep in your kitchen. (Most types can double as olive pitters.)

There are a couple of things to be aware

of when pitting cherries. First, they're going to splatter a bit, so be prepared, especially when pitting dark cherries that have deep scarlet juice. Also, unless you are extremely meticulous about accounting for every pit that comes from every cherry, be sure to check for pits later in the cooking process. There may be a stray pit that will wreak havoc on a tooth or become the source of unwelcome bits after a trip through the food processor. This concern holds true, too, for frozen or canned cherries, which generally have a warning to that effect on the label.

Peeling: For most stone fruit recipes, peeling the fruit isn't necessary. Typically the skin isn't thick or cumbersome in recipes, though when smoothness of texture or color is a goal the skin may need to be removed from the fruit. Peeling stone fruit follows the same technique used to peel tomatoes: Bring a pan of water to a boil, add the fruit and watch until you see the skin begin to split. This may take a matter of seconds or up to half a minute or so, depending on the variety of fruit and how ripe it is. Scoop out the fruit with a slotted spoon and run cold water over it to stop the cooking, and then simply slip the skin off.

Avoiding Discoloration: Many stone fruits will discolor to some degree after the flesh is exposed to the air, especially riper fruit. Discoloration can be more noticeable with pale varieties, such as Rainier cherries, which will be tinged with brown not long after being pitted. But even dark cherries will quickly change from deep purple to muddy purple brown if they sit around pitted or chopped before being used. And so I suggest in the recipes that the stone fruit be prepared just shortly before needed. And that's why acidic ingredients, such as lemon juice, appear often to help preserve the vivid color of the fruits. Once the fruit is submerged in liquid or tossed with other ingredients to help coat the exposed surfaces, discoloration will be greatly retarded.

Alternatives to Summer's Fresh Fruits

Though no off-season alternative can truly duplicate the peak-of-season experience we get from fresh stone fruit, on a gray, wintry day when you're eager for a taste of summer, frozen, dried, or canned fruit can provide a blissful moment. This is just the kind of experience Thierry Rautureau, chef-owner of Rover's restaurant in Seattle, has in mind for his customers when the kitchen staff spends countless summer hours canning perfectly ripe apricots, peaches, nectarines, and cherries. Throughout the summer season, he orders two boxes of each fruit weekly, using one fresh and canning the second. One recent summer they canned 175 pounds of Bing cherries, more than 100 pounds of nectarines and peaches, and about 70 pounds of apricots. Come winter, guests are marveling at the seared foie gras with apricots, the nectarine mousse cake, and the cherry clafoutis.

Some commercially frozen stone fruits are available, though selections will vary from region to region and store to store. Pitted dark sweet cherries are a good alternative for many recipes, not to mention a great convenience since the pitting has already been done. If using them in a recipe that calls for chopping the cherries, do so while they're frozen and firm; they'll soften up when fully thawed.

Freezing fruit at home requires dealing with the limitations of the average home freezer, which is better at keeping frozen foods frozen than freezing fresh foods because they are not nearly as cold as commercial freezers. Quick freezing at very low temperatures creates much smaller ice crystals than freezing at inconsistent or higher temperatures. Large ice crystals act like little daggers, puncturing the cell walls of foods and resulting in a much softer texture once thawed. A freezer that you're opening many times a day—fluctuating the temperature each time you open the door—will provide mediocre freezing results. Better is a chest freezer or other stand-alone freezer, used only for longer-term storage. Such freezers get less activity and typically maintain a lower temperature (by as much as 10 or 20°) than the freezer that's part of your refrigerator.

This is how I prefer to approach freezing fruit: start by pitting cherries and halving (or quartering) and pitting other stone fruits. Smaller fruits, such as cherries, apricots, and plums, can be frozen whole for convenience, though I do highly recommend pitting them first for even more convenience on the other end. Lay them in a single layer on a baking sheet with room between the pieces to ensure good circulation of the cold air. Freeze the fruit as is on the sheet until frozen solid; the timing will vary greatly with the size of the fruit pieces and the temperature of your freezer.

But don't be skimpy, give the fruit plenty of time to fully freeze, at least a few hours.

When the fruit is thoroughly frozen, transfer it to a durable resealable freezer bag and seal, expelling as much air from the bag as possible. Because the pieces were frozen separately, later you'll be able to easily remove and defrost only the amount of fruit you need. Don't forget to label the bag, as much for remembering the date you put them in the freezer as for what's in the bag. Frozen fruit won't have an indefinite life; it will be best if used within three or four months.

The most common dried stone fruits are apricots (primarily from Turkey but from California as well), cherries (Chukar is a favorite Northwest brand, see page 37), and prunes (mostly California). These fruits are wonderful off-season treats but can replace fresh fruit in more limited uses than frozen fruit. Plumping the fruit in warm water before using restores some of its bulk and tenderness but never really replicates the fresh form. The concentration of flavor and sweetness is, however, a welcome addition to many recipes, and can be preferable to fresh in recipes where that intensity of flavor is key.

Commercial canned fruits may be used for some recipes, but honestly they're not my favorite off-season choice. Because most are canned in syrup with varying levels of sweetness, knowing how much sugar to use in the recipe is hard to gauge. And it makes canned fruits not good candidates for savory recipes in which sugar is neither needed nor desired. If you're a canner, you might want to do as chef Rautureau does and put up some of the summer fruits to enjoy later in the year in sweet treats.

APRIL

Northwest Cherry Festival, The Dalles, Oregon

The last week of April each year, The Dalles on the Columbia River is home to a festival in honor of the region's long history of growing sweet cherries. At this time of year, the area's many orchards are in bloom—an impressive sight to behold—so you won't be munching on many cherries. But it's a great chance to visit the area and soak up the region's cherry culture while enjoying the festival activities, music, and carnival—with Saturday's big parade a special highlight. For more information, call 800-255-3385.

MAY

Prune Festival, Campbell, California

Not afraid to still call a prune a prune, the good people of Campbell host two days of festivities the third weekend of May to honor the region's prune-growing history, though today none of that industry remains in the area. That doesn't keep the town from celebrating its heritage, however, with a variety of festive events, not to mention plenty of prune-tasting opportunities, including efforts by celebrity chefs who come to show off their prune-cooking skills. For information, call 408-378-6252.

JUNE

Cherry Festival and Parade, San Leandro, California

You can count on many classic festival elements in San Leandro the first full weekend of June each year (the weekend following Memorial Day)—a community parade, live entertainment, arts and crafts booths among them—but the highlight of this festival is the Cherry Store where you can taste a variety of the season's sweet cherries in many forms, including salsas, jams, and chocolates. There's also a cherry pie bake-off and vendors serving up a wide array of cherry treats, so you're sure to get your quota of cherries. This festival originated back in 1906. For more information, call 510-577-3462 or go to www.ci.san-leandro.ca.us.

Cherry Festival, Yakima, Washington

Washington's Fruit Place, a visitor's center featuring information about the fruit industry in the Yakima Valley region, hosts a one-day cherry festival typically on the last Saturday of June each year. Visitors can sample the many varieties of cherries being harvested in these early days of the summer and collect information on the region's cherry growers and all types of cherry-related products. There are also kids' activities and other family-oriented fun. For more information, call 509-576-3090.

JULY

Cherry Time, Hood River Valley, Oregon

When cherry harvest begins in the valley, generally around the first of July, so begins a two-week celebration during which visitors to area cherry orchards can enjoy total immersion in the region's sweet cherries. Growers on the "Fruit Loop" pull out all the stops, offering cherry pies, cherry jams, cherry juices, U-pick cherry opportunities, and any number of other cherry products. For more information, go to www.hoodriverfruitloop.com or call 888-771-7327.

Cherry Fair, Kelowna, British Columbia

Mid- to late July each year (typically the third Saturday of the month), the British Columbia Orchard Industry Museum hosts a one-day fair featuring an up-close look at the region's cherry industry. Guests can taste a wide range of cherry varieties, from older heritage cherries to cherries more recently developed in the region. Everyone can enjoy the fun of the celebrity cherry pie bake-off and tasting products from area cottage industries (jams, juices, other interesting fruit products). For kids, there is an array of educational and craft activities, all pursuing a cherry theme. Call 250-763-0433 for more information or to confirm the date of the next fair.

AUGUST

Penticton Peach Festival, Penticton, British Columbia

The sandy, sunny shores at the south end of Lake Okanagan erupt in a peachy celebration the second weekend of August each year (beginning Wednesday, running through Sunday). The festival began in 1948, and today is a multigenerational family celebration. The festival's parade—the largest in British Columbia—is a main focus, but food lovers will want to check out the peach pie bake-off, as well as the peach pie-eating contest. For more information, go to www.peachfest.com or call 800-663-5052.

Peach-o-Rama, Seattle, Washington

Yes, this is a promotional peach celebration sponsored by a group of grocery stores, which typically wouldn't merit much attention. But what the Queen Anne Thriftways (in the Queen Anne and West Seattle neighborhoods, as well as in Tacoma) do each year is noteworthy in raising consumers' awareness that all peaches aren't created equal. Throughout the few weeks (timing depends on the peaches but often beginning in late July and continuing to mid-August), shoppers can sample the peaches on the spot or in a number of dishes available for tasting. There are also special events including celebrity chef demonstrations and a chance to meet the growers. For details, go to www.peachorama.com or call the Peach-o-Rama hotline at 206-933-9475.

SEPTEMBER

Dried Plum Festival, Yuba City, California

The weekend after Labor Day each year, this Central Valley city celebrates the significant impact that the prune (officially now called the dried plum) has had on California agriculture, with a weekend of live music, celebrity chef demonstrations, and plum industry representatives sharing all they know about this important agricultural product. For more information, go to www.driedplumfestival.org or call 530-671-3100.

ONGOING

The Hood River Fruit Loop, Oregon

Beginning in the city of Hood River on the banks of the Columbia River, this loop drive guides you through about 45 scenic miles of this lush and productive valley. A couple dozen spots are on the self-guided itinerary, including farms, orchards, and fruit markets. Though many of these places are open year-round, several special events are planned each year, from the late-April Blossom Festival through the autumn tradition of Harvest Fest in late October. For information, go to www.hoodriverfruitloop.com or call 888-771-7327.

Luther Burbank Experiment Farm, Sebastopol, California

You can visit the farm where famed horticulturist Luther Burbank did much of his experimentation with fruit and other cultivars, with many examples on the property. The farm, also known as the Gold Ridge Farm, is associated with the Western Sonoma County Historical Society, preserving the heritage of the region, which certainly includes some distinctive agricultural traditions. For information, call 707-829-6711 or go to www.wschs-grf.pon.net.

Washington's Fruit Place, Yakima, Washington

This visitor's center in downtown Yakima (105 South 18th Street) is a resource for plenty of information about the fruit growing of this region, with displays relating to the agriculture industry as well as samples of seasonal fruits when they are being harvested in the area. Call 509-576-3090 for more information.

FARMERS MARKETS ONLINE

www.ams.usda.gov/farmersmarkets

The U.S. Department of Agriculture's Agricultural Marketing Service offers a comprehensive online resource of farmers markets throughout the country, organized by state.

www.bcfarmersmarket.org

The British Columbia Association of Farmers Markets has a Web site that offers resources to help track down markets in that province, as well as lots of other information about farming in the region.

www.portlandfarmersmarket.org

This Web site provides information on the weekly farmers markets held in Portland, generally May through October.

www.seattlefarmersmarkets.org

Information on the weekly farmers markets held in Seattle, generally late May through October, can be found here.

www.eatlocal.org

Information on neighborhood farmers markets held in Vancouver, British Columbia, generally mid-May through mid-October, can be found here.